ADVANCED
CALCULATOR
MATH

Gerardus Vervoort • Dale J. Mason

A FEARON
MAKEMASTER® BOOK

FEARON PITMAN PUBLISHERS, INC.
Belmont, California

The Calculator Math Series:
   Beginning Calculator Math (Book 1)
   Intermediate Calculator Math (Book 2)
   Advanced Calculator Math (Book 3)

Consultant: Alan Ovson
Cover designer: Susan True
Editorial and graphic services: Sheridan Publications Services,
   Nevada City, California

Note: *Beginning Calculator Math, Intermediate Calculator Math,* and *Advanced Calculator Math* are based on *Calculator Activities for the Classroom 1, 2, and 3* (ditto master books), and *Calculator Activities for the Classroom: Teacher's Resource Book,* published by Copp Clark Publishing, a division of Copp Clark Limited, Toronto, Canada. Some additional activity sheets may be found in the original publications, which are available from Copp Clark Publishing, 517 Wellington Street West, Toronto, Ontario, Canada, M5V 1G1.

ISBN-0-8224-1202-0

Printed in the United States of America.

1.9 8 7 6 5 4 3 2 1

Preface

I have always endeavoured according to my strength and the measure of my ability to do away with the difficulty and tediousness of calculations, the irksomeness of which is wont to deter very many from the study of mathematics.

John Napier
From the *Dedication of Rabdologiae*

This comment by the inventor of logarithms still applies today. Manipulation of numbers is not the prime objective of an arithmetic program—in fact, it is only a minor part. People must know *when* to multiply and subtract as well as know *how* to multiply and subtract. They also must know what information is required to solve a problem and whether a proposed answer is reasonable.

Problem solving in the broadest sense is the essence of mathematics, and it is here that we find the calculator's value to the mathematics program. With the calculator eliminating the drudgery of lengthy calculations, the student can concentrate on the problem-solving process. Here are some specific situations where the calculator is useful:

— Estimating—mentally grasping the overall proportions of an operation—is an essential skill. The calculator enables students to make estimates and then rapidly get feedback on their correctness. Interestingly, while the calculator facilitates development of estimating skills, using a calculator also increases the need for that ability, for minor operating slips or use of a calculator with a low battery can easily produce incorrect answers. Users must thus develop a feeling for what the answer to a problem should be, and critically examine the answers that are displayed. *Elementary Calculator Math, Intermediate Calculator Math,* and *Advanced Calculator Math* each contains a series of activities to improve the students' ability to find approximate answers to addition, subtraction, multiplication, and division problems. Note that many educators differentiate between *estimation* and *approximation*, and the distinction may be useful. We have chosen to use the term *estimation* to cover both meanings. Those wishing to help their students learn both terms are encouraged to do so.

— Problem solving using mathematics is enhanced by use of the calculator. Students (and others) have often been dissuaded from attacking some types of problems because of the length of the computations involved. The calculator frees them to concentrate on what information is required to solve a problem, what steps and operations are involved, and what answers are reasonable. The *Intermediate* and *Advanced* books, in particular, show how both everyday problems and more intricate mathematical ones (too cumbersome for paper and pencil solution) can be handled easily with the aid of the calculator.

— Understanding of fractions can be enhanced by use of the calculator. It can also be used to develop the concept of a fraction and the relationship between common and decimal fractions. Calculator algorithms can be developed for operations with fractions. It should be noted that in spite of emphasis on the metric system and the increased emphasis on decimal fractions, common fractions have not disappeared entirely (nor should they). Not only is the concept of 1/3 much easier to grasp than $0.\overline{3}$, but students in the intermediate grades must be prepared to deal with algebra of the form $\frac{a+b}{c}$. Also, fractions provide opportunities for students to think their way through various calculator algorithms. The *Intermediate* and *Advanced* books contain many activities that use common and decimal fractions. A series of exercises is included to help students perform operations such as 3/4 + 5/8 on the calculator.

— Detecting and identifying patterns is the essence of inductive reasoning. The calculator can be the "number laboratory" where the student performs a series of numerical experiments, develops a hypothesis, and checks the conclusion by further experiments. In the past, these types of exercises, though recognized as desirable, were impossible due to the drudgery of the required computations. Many activities on patterns in all three *Calculator Math* books provide opportunities for students and teachers to engage in this type of experimentation.

— All teachers know that games, tricks, and puzzles help motivate students. They can be used to drill facts, expand concepts, and provide opportunities for discovery. Therefore, each book of *Calculator Math* contains a section of games and similar activities for individuals, small groups, or whole classes.

The *Calculator Math* books have been created to make connections between the calculator's capabilities, the learning of concepts in mathematics, and the application of those concepts and the calculator's capabilities to realistic problems. The flexible MAKEMASTER® duplicatable format enables any of the activity sheets to be used in multiple copies with minimal expense. The teacher's guide and skill-and-topic annotations on the activity sheets help connect the activities to the mathematics curriculum. Many of the activities suggested on the sheets can be continued with similar material provided by the teacher or invented by the students. We urge teachers to go further than we have, to build even more activities for their classes. They will enrich their mathematics program by doing so; they will help their students productively use one of the technological marvels of the twentieth century; and they will mightily please Mr. Napier's ghost besides!

The Authors

Note: Materials and literature on calculator applications in the mathematics program are rapidly proliferating. Readers who wish to pursue the subject in greater depth are advised to write the Calculator Information Center, 1200 Chambers Road, Columbus, Ohio 43212 (Telephone 614-422-8509). The center publishes a regular bulletin, free of charge, listing available materials and other resources.

Contents

Activities Overview

Activity Category:	Activity sheet numbers in:		
	Beginning Calculator Math	Intermediate Calculator Math	Advanced Calculator Math
Learning About the Calculator	1—10	1—8	1—5
Estimation	11—31	9—20	6—9
Games	32—42	21—28	10—15
Fractions		29—32	16—20
Patterns	43—44	33—34	21—30
Problem Solving	45—52	35—43	31—43
Content Lessons		44—47	44—46

Note: For ease of reference and to avoid the implications that *Beginning, Intermediate,* and *Advanced* may have for students, the teacher's notes and MAKEMASTER® activity sheets in the three *Calculator Math* books carry a double number. The first number indicates the book (*1-* denotes sheets in the *Beginning* book, *2-* sheets in the *Intermediate* book, and *3-* sheets in the *Advanced* book). The second number gives the activity-sheet number within that book. Thus, *2-14* indicates activity sheet 14 in the *Intermediate* book.

Topics-and-Skills Overview

Topics/Skills	Beginning Calculator Math (Book 1) Sheet numbers	Intermediate Calculator Math (Book 2) Sheet numbers	Advanced Calculator Math (Book 3) Sheet numbers
Calculator Mechanics			
familiarization with the calculator	1, 2, 3, 4, 5, 6, 7, 8, 10		1, 2, 3
speed and accuracy with the calculator	2, 3, 4, 5, 6, 7, 8, 10		
optimum use of the calculator		1, 2, 3, 4, 5, 6, 8	1, 2, 3, 4, 5, 18, 19 20, 35
judicious use of the calculator	9		32
special calculator algorithms	41		18, 19, 20, 44, 45, 46
Whole Numbers			
addition facts	2, 6, 7, 8, 10, 32, 37 38, 39	22	
subtraction facts	3, 6, 7, 8, 10, 33, 37 38, 39		
multiplication facts	4, 6, 7, 8, 10, 37, 38 39	1, 24, 26	10, 11
division facts	5, 6, 7, 8, 10, 37, 38 39, 40	24	10
order of operations	41	1, 8	
Estimation			
rounding	11, 12, 13, 14, 15, 16, 17–27, 28–31	10–21	6, 8, 9
estimation, addition	11, 12, 13, 14, 15, 16 48	9, 10, 11, 35	6
estimation, subtraction	17, 18, 19, 20, 34		6, 14
estimation, multiplication	21–27, 34, 35	12–19, 23, 25, 26, 36, 37, 41, 42	7, 8, 11, 13, 14
estimation, division	29, 30, 31, 35, 36	20, 21, 26	9, 11
large numbers		43	41, 42
using estimation to solve equations		45, 46	

Topics/Skills	Beginning Calculator Math (Book 1) Sheet numbers	Intermediate Calculator Math (Book 2) Sheet numbers	Advanced Calculator Math (Book 3) Sheet numbers
Common/Decimal Fractions			
concepts		29, 44	
equivalent fractions		29, 30, 31, 32	16, 17
converting, fractions/ decimals		29, 30, 31, 32	16, 17
operations with fractions	28		18, 19, 20
Problems			
using intuition		33, 34	
developing strategies	32, 33, 34, 35, 36, 38 39		42
developing mathematical reasoning			30, 44, 45, 46
solving problems	45, 46, 47, 49, 51, 52	35, 36, 37, 38, 39, 40, 41, 42, 43	4, 5, 15
Patterns			
detecting/completing	33, 34, 35, 36, 43, 44	23, 33, 34, 44	21, 22, 23, 24, 25, 26, 27, 28, 29, 30
explaining		44	22, 23, 24, 25, 26, 27
Handling Data			
reading/constructing tables, graphs, diagrams	14, 47, 48	39, 40	31, 35, 36, 37
gathering/organizing data	45, 46	35, 37, 41, 42, 47	12, 15, 31, 34, 36, 37, 39
data and averages		22, 41, 42	12, 33, 34, 36, 37
Rate, Ratio, Percent			
rate, ratio, percent	49, 50, 51, 52	38, 41, 42	32, 34, 35, 36, 37, 38, 39, 40, 42
interest			1, 2, 4, 5
taxation			3, 31
consumer awareness	45, 46, 47, 49, 50	35, 36, 37, 38	1, 2, 3, 4, 5, 31, 32, 36

Topics/Skills	Beginning Calculator Math (Book 1) Sheet numbers	Intermediate Calculator Math (Book 2) Sheet numbers	Advanced Calculator Math (Book 3) Sheet numbers
Measurement			
linear measurement	49—52	38—42	
volume		38, 39, 41, 42	
area	49, 50, 51, 52	39, 40	
time		43	
Other Concepts			
number properties		5, 6, 7, 8, 44	18, 25, 26, 27
factors/multiples	36	24	10, 15
exponents, squares/square roots		4, 25	14, 22, 23, 24
limits			7, 28, 29, 39
pi		39, 47	40
negative integers		2	6
developing algebraic reasoning	42	27, 28, 45, 46	25, 26, 27, 43
inverse operations			44, 45, 46
significant digits	31	44	

Teacher's Guide

NOTE: Some Recommendations for Calculator Purchases

To many people, a calculator is a calculator. However, there are great differences between different brands and models of calculators. These differences include the type of logic employed, which dictates the order in which keys must be struck. Other differences are: available functions (%, $\sqrt{}$, and so on); size of display; automatic/manual constant; floating/fixed decimal point; automatic display shut-off; size; spacing and arrangement of keys; sturdiness of case; durability; and power source.

Selection of a particular model depends on the grade levels of the students who will be using the machine, and on the purposes of the program. Features that seem mandatory for calculators intended for intermediate school students include: sturdiness; algebraic mode (natural order arithmetic); floating decimal point; 8-digit display; automatic constant.

Rechargeable batteries are (or were) a frequent cause of breakdown. Moreover, depending on the recharging mechanism, the constant connection of rundown units to an external power source can be a nuisance. On the other hand, replacement batteries can be very costly in the long run.

Due to the large number of variations among calculators, it is most desirable that all students in the elementary classroom use the same model.

Five Activity Sheets for Learning About the Calculator*

3-1 The Cost of Money: Part I

Focus on . . .

- *Introducing the % key*
- *Using the calculator effectively*
- *Building consumer awareness*

Extension

Discuss the differences in interest rates for borrowing money and investing money (such as in a savings account). Have students find the amount of interest they would *pay* to borrow $2000 at 9%, at 10%, at 12.5%, and at 18%. Then have students find the amount of interest they would *earn* in a savings account on $2000 at 4%, at 5%, at 5.5%, and at 6%. Point out the importance of shopping for the "best" interest rate whether borrowing money or investing it.

3-2 The Cost of Money: Part II

Focus on . . .

- *Introducing the % key*
- *Using the calculator effectively*
- *Building consumer awareness*

Note

Before calculating simple interest for more than a one-year period, check students' calculators. Some may have an automatic constant that helps to figure interest for periods greater than one year.

Extension

Have students translate different per-month interest charges into yearly rates and calculate payments required for yearly or monthly periods.

3-3 The State's Little Bit Extra

Focus on . . .

- *Using the % key*
- *Understanding taxation*

Note

Students should be familiar with the percent key and aware that (in most states) sales tax is levied on certain categories of purchases.

Extensions

1. On any problem that deals with the purchase of goods, ask students to calculate sales tax. Have students make up problems for each other, using the proper tax rate for your locality.
2. Discuss the state's use of sales tax revenues.

*For solutions, see *Answer Key*, pp. 58—60.

3-4 Money, Money in the Bank: Part I

Focus on . . .
- *Using the % key*
- *Understanding compound interest*
- *Using the calculator effectively*

Notes

1. For Problem 2, the calculator may be keyed in one of two ways:

or

However, the first keying works only if the first number entered is the multiplicative constant. Students who have calculators operating with the second number as the constant should key the number 100 first, then 1.07. This sequence is shown on sheet 3-5, Problem 1, Method B. Give students additional answers in the series and ask them to work out the keying sequence that produces those answers.

2. Many students find this work difficult, so a slower pace may be required.

Extension

Discuss the surprising speed with which compound interest adds up.

3-5 Money, Money in the Bank: Part II

Focus on . . .
- *Using the % key*
- *Understanding compound interest*

Note

Method B will not work as given for calculators that operate with the first number entered as the multiplicative constant. However, most students are able to discover the keying sequence required for such calculators. Ask your students to *estimate* the first several answers for Method B before using the calculator; absurd answers from an inappropriate keying sequence will then be quickly spotted.

Four Activity Sheets on Estimation*

3-6 How Fast Can You Estimate?

Focus on . . .
- *Reviewing estimation and rounding*
- *Rounding to the nearest five or ten*
- *Estimating positive and negative integers*

Note

Students need to be acquainted with negative integers before doing these exercises. Students can record exact answers in the right margin.

3-7 Smaller, Smaller, Smaller

Focus on . . .
- *Estimating in multiplication*
- *Developing the concept of limits*

Note

This exercise provides the opportunity for the student to develop an intuitive concept of limit.

Extension

Students may be challenged to work out the rule for deciding which triangles are the most "Bermuda" (i.e., those which disappear with the fewest operations).

3-8 All-Star Estimating

Focus on . . .
- *Rounding with decimals*
- *Estimating in multiplication*

Notes

1. Students must understand significant digits.
2. Students must be able to round decimal fractions.
3. Use sheet 2-44 (*Intermediate Calculator Math*) to prepare students in placing decimal points.

3-9 Divide and Figure

Focus on . . .
- *Reviewing estimation in division*
- *Rounding in division*

Note

Students may be tempted to resort to their calculators before completing their estimations. Emphasize that the calculator is to be used only for checking the estimated answers.

*For solutions, see *Answer Key*, pp. 60—62.

Six Activity Sheets with Games

3-10 Factor Finesse

Focus on . . .

- *Practicing multiplication and division facts*
- *Factoring*

Notes

1. Students should understand the concept of factors.
2. A more permanent spinner may be made by gluing the spinner shown to a small piece of plywood and driving a short common nail into the center. Use a hairpin as the spinner.

Extension

Variations to the game (listed on the sheet) should not be attempted until students are very familiar with the original game.

3-11 Name Your Numbers

Focus on . . .

- *Practicing estimation with multiplication and division facts*

Note

Players should alternate in choosing destination numbers.

3-12 The "Get Mean" Game

Focus on . . .

- *Collecting data*
- *Estimating an average*

Note

Students should know how to calculate an average.

Extension

Students can order the values entered to make a frequency distribution by writing them down at the same time they are keyed into the calculator. Then they can identify the *median* weight, the *mode*, and the *range* of the weights. The data could also be used to make a bar graph.

3-13 Right On!

Focus on . . .

- *Estimating a factor with precision*
- *Multiplying with decimal fractions*

Note

Some calculators may not operate with the first number entered as the multiplicative constant, and so the keying sequence shown will not work. Newer calculators are usually capable of storing the starting number in the memory, with the Memory Recall key being used to retrieve it for each try. With other calculators the starting number will have to be rekeyed for each try.

3-14 Pretty Square

Focus on . . .

- *Estimating in multiplication and division*
- *Finding square roots*

Notes

1. Students should be familiar with the basic concept of square root before attempting this game.
2. Students can be challenged to find different ways of checking their estimate using the calculator.

3-15 Animal, Vegetable, or Numeral?

Focus on . . .

- *Gathering data*
- *Using factors and multiples*
- *Developing problem-solving strategies*

Notes

1. Homogeneous grouping of four or five students may work best for this game.
2. The teacher may want to help students focus on the *types* of questions that can be used, even though these are suggested in the example.

Five Activity Sheets on Fractions*

3-16 A Decimal by Another Name

Focus on . . .

- *Converting decimals to fractions*
- *Working with equivalent fractions*

Note

Some classes may benefit from having more examples than could be included on the sheet. You may want to move through the sheet step-by-step with the entire class, adding the additional examples as students indicate a need for them.

*For solutions, see *Answer Key*, pp. 62—65.

3-17 It's All Equal

Focus on . . .

- *Converting fractions to decimals*
- *Working with equivalent fractions*

Note

The correct method of changing 3/5 to 15/25 is to change 3/5 to a decimal, and then change the decimal to a fraction with the denominator of 25. The keying sequence is:

$$\boxed{3}\ \boxed{\div}\ \boxed{5}\ \boxed{\times}\ \boxed{2}\ \boxed{5}\ \boxed{=}\ \boxed{\qquad 15}$$

(display)

This can be shown algebraically as:

$$\frac{3}{5} = \frac{x}{25}$$

$$\frac{3}{5} \times 25 = \frac{x}{25} \times 25$$

$$\boxed{3 \div 5 \times 25} = x$$

3-18 The Calculating Fraction: Part I

3-19 The Calculating Fraction: Part II

Focus on . . .

- *Adding and subtracting common fractions*
- *Using the calculator optimally*
- *Working with the distributive property*
- *Working with calculator algorithms*

Notes

Students should work through Exercises A, B, and C without using calculators. Present the following minilesson after students have completed Exercise C.

1. Have students work Problem 1 in Exercise C by changing the fractions to decimals and then adding, using only the calculator. It may seem possible to solve Problem 1 this way:

$$\boxed{3}\ \boxed{\div}\ \boxed{4}\ \boxed{+}\ \boxed{7}\ \boxed{\div}\ \boxed{8}\ \boxed{=}$$

Ask students to try this method and write down the answer. They should repeat the same kind of keying sequence for Problem 2. Ask students to compare the answers obtained with the answers they obtained in working the problem without using the calculator.

2. Examine the problems with students. Explain that although

$$\boxed{3}\ \boxed{\div}\ \boxed{4}\ \boxed{+}\ \boxed{7}\ \boxed{\div}\ \boxed{8}\ \boxed{=}$$

appears to be a correct string of operations, the fact that the calculator operates on all preceding results as it goes along means that the final keying (divide by 8) tells the machine to divide all its work up to that point by 8, even though the operator's intent was only that 7 be divided by 8.

3. Students can add a *compensating* step: If they multiply 3 ÷ 4 by 8 in advance, then divide by 8 later on, the two operations will "undo" each other and the correct answer can be obtained from the calculator. On paper it would look like this: [(3 ÷ 4) × 8) + 7] ÷ 8, instead of like this: (3 ÷ 4) + (7 ÷ 8). Have them try Problem 2 in Exercise C for practice. They should punch in:

$$\boxed{1}\ \boxed{\div}\ \boxed{2}\ \boxed{\times}\ \boxed{1}\ \boxed{6}\ \boxed{+}\ \boxed{7}\ \boxed{\div}\ \boxed{1}\ \boxed{6}$$

The correct answer is 0.9375.

4. Now have students complete Exercise D on their calculators using the compensating step.

5. Sheet 3-19 is an expansion of sheet 3-18. It uses the compensating step described in *Note* 3 above.

3-20 Fast Fractions

Focus on . . .

- *Using the calculator optimally*
- *Multiplying fractions*
- *Working with calculator algorithms*

Note

Before proceeding with Exercise B, the following minilesson should be presented.

Have students find 3/4 × 7 on their calculators. There are four ways in which this may be done:

- **a.** 3 ÷ 4 × 7 = 5.25
- **b.** 7 ÷ 4 × 3 = 5.25
- **c.** 3 × 7 ÷ 4 = 5.25
- **d.** 7 × 3 ÷ 4 = 5.25

Methods **c** and **d** always give the same results on all calculators. However, under special circumstances **a** may give a different result than **b**, and **b** may give a different result than **c**. This is due to the machine's habit of cutting off decimals when a result exceeds storage capacity. The technical term for this is *truncation*.

Ten Activity Sheets on Patterns*

3-21 Be a Number Detective: Part I

Focus on . . .
- *Detecting and completing patterns*

Note

Some students may be unable to detect a pattern after three items. Have them try the first prediction still using the calculator before attempting to make a prediction about the remaining items.

3-22 Be a Number Detective: Part II

Focus on . . .
- *Detecting and completing patterns*
- *Explaining patterns*
- *Squaring and square root*

Notes

1. Previous experience with geoboards and pegboards is very helpful.
2. The squares of dots show a geometric justification for an algebraic sum. By dividing the squares as shown, each section represents one of the terms in the sum, while the square itself represents the sum. The length of the side of the square equals the number of terms. Therefore, (the number of terms)² equals the sum. For example, the sum $1 + 3 + 5 + 7 + 9 + 11 + 13 + 15$ has 8 terms. Thus,

$$1 + 3 + 5 + 7 + 9 + 11 + 13 + 15 = 8^2 = 64$$

Extension

Note 2 above provides the basis for finding a formula for the sum $1 + 3 + 5 + \ldots + n$. Students only need to find a way to express the number of terms. *Answer:* $\left(\dfrac{1+n}{2}\right)^2 = \text{sum}$

3-23 Be a Square Detective

Focus on . . .
- *Detecting and explaining patterns*
- *Squaring and square root*

Note

It is helpful to have squared paper available for this exercise; turning the paper to a 45° angle helps students arrange dots in a symmetric pattern.

*For solutions, see *Answer Key*, pp. 65–70.

3-24 The Three-Angle Detective

Focus on . . .
- *Detecting and completing patterns*
- *Explaining patterns*
- *Squaring and square root*

Note

As for sheet 3-23, it is helpful to have squared paper available.

3-25 Pattern Power

Focus on . . .
- *Detecting patterns*
- *Explaining patterns*
- *Understanding number properties*
- *Developing algebraic reasoning*

Extension

After they have completed the sheet, have students find and explain some patterns of their own.

3-26 More Pattern Power

Focus on . . .
- *Detecting patterns*
- *Explaining patterns*
- *Understanding number properties*
- *Developing algebraic reasoning*

Extension

After the students have explained the patterns, have them choose a number that can be multiplied by any *two-digit* number to make those two digits repeat several times. To do this, they can compare their work on Problems 1 and 2 to that on Problem 3. Alternatively, they can create a repeating number such as 434343 on the calculator display and divide by the two digits that repeat (in this case, 43). *Answer:* 10101 or 1010101.

Then have them factor the number to write a problem similar to Problem 1.

3-27 Super Pattern Power

Focus on . . .
- *Detecting patterns*
- *Explaining patterns*
- *Understanding number properties*
- *Developing algebraic reasoning*

Extension

After they have completed the sheet, have students find some patterns of their own and challenge other students to explain them.

3-28 Just a Little Bit Closer

Focus on . . .

- *Detecting patterns*
- *Conceptualizing limits*

Note

Introduce the phrase "the sequence approaches 1" or "the sequence tends to 1" to describe what is happening.

3-29 How Close Can You Get?

Focus on . . .

- *Detecting patterns*
- *Conceptualizing limits*
- *Understanding convergent sequence*

Note

Again introduce the phrase "the sequence approaches 1" or "the sequence tends to 1 (or another number)" as a description of the pattern being observed.

Extension

Show students how to write the sequence in Problem 1 in general form:

$$\frac{n+1}{n}, \text{ where } n = 1, 2, 3, \ldots$$

Then have them write their answers for Problems 5 and 6 in general form.

Possible answers:

5. $\frac{1}{n+1}$, where $n = 1, 2, 3, \ldots$

6. $\frac{n}{2n+1}$, where $n = 1, 2, 3, \ldots$

3-30 Paper Folding Challenge

Focus on . . .

- *Detecting patterns*
- *Developing mathematical reasoning*

Note

Each student will need several sheets of folding paper (old dittoes will do). Encourage students to discover a pattern rather than counting parts and creases.

Extension

Have students write the formulas for the values in the tables.

Answers:

1. Number of parts = $p + 1$, where p = number of points.
2. Number of parts = 2^n, where n = number of times folded; number of creases = $2^n - 1$, where n = number of times folded.
3. Number of parts = 2^n, where n = number of times folded; number of crease lines = n, where n = number of times folded.

*Thirteen Activity Sheets on Problem Solving**

3-31 The New You

Focus on . . .

- *Gathering data*
- *Constructing tables*
- *Computing tax*

Note

Ads from newspapers can be used as well as department store catalogs.

3-32 Best Buys

Focus on . . .

- *Working with ratio*
- *Building consumer awareness*
- *Using the calculator judiciously*

Note

This may be a good time to discuss economic concepts such as price competition, loss leaders, and the costs and benefits of advertising. A chart of the distances between major markets may make it clear why it is often uneconomical to try to save by finding the best buys wherever they may be located.

3-33 Batter Up!

Focus on . . .

- *Finding and evaluating averages*
- *Discerning the basis for an average*

Note

The criteria for answers to Questions 1 and 2 can be discussed. Why, for instance, is Brown better to have on your team than Kolinski? The definition

*For solutions, see *Answer Key*, pp. 70–76.

of a "batting average" precludes averaging the individual averages to get the team average, although it might appear that the latter strategy would work. Have students compute the "average of the averages" and compare this answer to the team average. Ask them to explain why the average of the averages is lower. (The answer is that the higher-average players are at bat proportionately more of the time, so their efforts raise the overall average. An average of the individual averages would err on the low side.)

3-34 If the Shoe Fits . . .

Focus on . . .
- *Gathering data*
- *Finding averages*
- *Finding ratios*

Extension

Challenge students to find other common items with similar easily identifiable components (buttons on shirts, for example), and work out assumptions and operations for calculating national totals.

3-35 Faster Than a Speeding Snail

Focus on . . .
- *Calculating ratios*
- *Constructing graphs*
- *Using constants*

Notes

1. As students arrange the animals in order of speed (Problem a), they should write the results in the spaces to the left of the bar graph.
2. Students should be aware that ratios can be expressed as decimals (for example, 63:45 = 1.40).
3. The most efficient method of computing the ratio is to program the calculator constant to divide by 45, by keying:

3-36 Pop Pop and Fizz Fizz

Focus on . . .
- *Gathering data*
- *Finding averages and ratios*
- *Building consumer awareness*
- *Reading and constructing tables*

Extension

Students can research figures (perhaps with the help of a home economist at a supermarket chain or consumer center) on the cost of the various components of the year's supply of pop—sugar, water, flavoring, cans, and so on.

3-37 A Day in Your Life

Focus on . . .
- *Gathering data*
- *Finding averages*
- *Finding percentages*
- *Reading and constructing tables*

Extension

The tables, when completed, are a good basis for constructing circle graphs.

3-38 Kool-Punch and Cake

Focus on . . .
- *Finding ratios and percentages*
- *Working with metric quantities*

Extension

Have students find the current prices for the ingredients of the cake in Problem 2. Then have them calculate the cost of the 11,365 kg cake.

3-39 Money Matters

Focus on . . .
- *Collecting data*
- *Finding the mass of an object*
- *Conceptualizing a limit*
- *Finding rates*

Note

For the first problem students will need to know or find out the current cost of a commonly smoked cigarette. For the second problem they'll need an accurate scale and a number of coins.

Extensions

1. Students can compute how many bicycles, pairs of jeans, and so on, could be purchased with the money saved by not smoking for *x* number of years.
2. Have students find out how much they would be worth if they were worth their weight in pennies, dimes, nickels, or quarters.

3-40 Round Things

Focus on . . .

- *Working with pi*
- *Working with ratios*
- *Finding rates of speed*

Note

Have students use $355 \div 113$ to compute π to 6 significant figures.

Extension

Students can make up similar problems for each other based on catalog sources, the *Guinness Book of Records*, and so on.

3-41 Moo!

Focus on . . .

- *Working with large numbers*
- *Working with ratios*

Note

Useful metric understandings for this sheet are: 1000 milliliters equals 1 liter or, in volume terms, 1 cubic decimeter. Or, 1 milliliter equals 1 cubic centimeter. That is: 1000 mL = 1 L; 1 mL = 1 cc.

3-42 From One Small Piece

Focus on . . .

- *Sampling a large population*
- *Developing problem-solving strategies*
- *Working with ratios*

Notes

1. Students must realize that only about 0.6 of this page has names. Since there are approximately 50 names in one of these columns, a full page would contain $50 \times 3 \div 0.6 = 250$ names.
2. In order to answer Question 1b, students will have to construct an assumption about the number of persons per telephone in this city. Two per phone is a reasonable start, although the class could do a survey of itself as another way of arriving at a figure.
3. Estimates of the number of businesses may be inaccurate because of the limited sampling; accuracy can be increased by sampling a variety of pages at random.

Extension

The same exercise, with more varied samples, can be tried with your local phone book. If interested,

students can usually check the accuracy of their findings by calling the telephone company.

3-43 Friends

Focus on . . .

- *Developing algebraic reasoning*

Note

During the discussion, students may be able to see similarities between the two situations. A handshake between two people corresponds to the two giving each other a present. There will be twice as many presents as handshakes.

Three Activity Sheets with Content Lessons*

3-44 Remainders and the Calculator: Part I

Focus on . . .

- *Developing calculator algorithms*
- *Developing mathematical reasoning*
- *Reviewing inverse operations*

Notes

1. Allow students some tinker time to find an algorithm for determining the whole remainder from the decimal quotient.
2. Ask students to find the elements that must be used in the longhand-decimal problems if they are to compute the remainder from the decimal quotient. Present more examples if necessary.

3-45 Remainders and the Calculator: Part II

Focus on . . .

- *Developing calculator algorithms*
- *Developing mathematical reasoning*
- *Reviewing inverse operations*

Notes

1. Review sheet 3-44 if it has not been done immediately preceding.
2. Have students work Exercises 1 and 2 on the sheet.
3. Give additional help with the sequence shown for Exercise 2, if required, by going through this

*For solutions, see *Answer Key*, pp. 76—77.

problem on the calculator:

Step	Press	Display
1	(1)(1)(4)	114
2	(÷)	114
3	(1)(6)	16
4	(=)	7.125
5	(−)	7.125
6	(7)	0.125
7	(×)	0.125
8	(1)(6)	16
9	(=)	2

4. Check answers to Exercise 3 to make sure students have consistently followed the proper sequence of operations.

3-46 Remainders and the Calculator: Part III

Focus on . . .
- *Developing calculator algorithms*
- *Developing mathematical reasoning*
- *Reviewing inverse operations*

Notes

1. Review sheet 3-44 if not done recently.
2. Have the class do Exercises 1 through 4.
3. Discuss what happens inside a calculator when it is presented with a problem such as $(1 \div 3) \times 3$, and why the answer is 0.9999999 instead of 1. The process is called *truncation*. Better and more expensive calculators give the answer as 1.
4. Problems 1 and 3 are the same. Which answers do your students think are correct? Most calculators simply forget about all digits after the one on the right of the display. The answer on the machine is, therefore, a little bit wrong. When that answer is multiplied by 3, the machine shows 0.9999999. The correct answer is 1, but the calculator's answer is very, very close. Remind the students that when the calculator shows 0.9999999 it usually means 1.

3-1

The Cost of Money: Part I

Simple interest—how much you pay

Work through the following example.

Example 1		**Solution**
Deposit or Loan (Principal) :	$100	8% of $100 = 0.08 × $100 = $8
Interest Rate :	8%	Interest = $8
Interest after 1 year = _____		Total owing = $100 (principal) + $8 (interest)
Total owing after 1 year = _____		= $108

The calculator is able to do this type of question. Look at Example 1 again. Punch in:

$\boxed{1}$ $\boxed{0}$ $\boxed{0}$ $\boxed{+}$ $\boxed{8}$ $\boxed{\%}$ The display shows "8." This is the interest. Push $\boxed{=}$ The display shows "108." This is the total (principal + interest). Try Example 1 again.

It is possible to find the total (principal + interest) in one step, without using the % key. For Example 1, the steps would be: $\boxed{1}$ $\boxed{0}$ $\boxed{0}$ $\boxed{\times}$ $\boxed{1}$ $\boxed{.}$ $\boxed{0}$ $\boxed{8}$ $\boxed{=}$

100% (principal) + 8% (interest)

The display would read "108," the total.
By subtracting the principal (100), you can find the interest (108 − 100 = 8).

1.
Principal :	$250
Interest Rate :	9%
Interest :	_____
Total Owing (after 1 year) :	_____

2. Find the value after 1 year of :

$87.49 invested at 9% : _____

$2645 invested at 12% : _____

3.

Principal	Rate	Interest	Total After 1 year
$ 460.00	4%	_____	_____
$ 625.49	9%	_____	_____
$4000.00	11%	_____	_____
$ 256.33	7%	_____	_____
$5847.00	9.5%	_____	_____

• *Introducing the % key*
• *Using the calculator effectively*
• *Building consumer awareness*

Name _____

3-2

The Cost of Money: Part II

More on calculating simple interest

Advanced Calculator Math

Money is often borrowed or deposited for longer periods of time. In these cases, simple interest is computed on the original amount (the principal) every year.

Example		**Solution**

Example

Principal :	$300
Interest Rate :	6%
Loan Period :	4 years
Interest per year :	_____
Interest for 4 years :	_____
Interest + principal :	_____

Solution

Interest for 1 year = $300 × 0.06
= $18
Interest for 4 years = $18 × 4
= $72
Total = $300 + $72
= $372

Fast Method

Push   ③   ⓪   ⓪   ⊞   ⑥   ⅏   ⊟   ⊟   ⊟   ⊟

4 years

1. Interest Rate :   14%   **$867.99**
     Period :   2 years
   Total Payable : _____

2. Interest Rate :   7%   **$2469.00 (savings account)**
     Period :   4 years
  Total after 4 years : _____

3.

Principal	Rate	Period	Interest	Total Payable
$ 420.25	12 %	3 years	_____	_____
$1200.72	9.5%	5 years	_____	_____
$1935.72	14 %	15 years	_____	_____
$ 318.75	10 %	12 years	_____	_____
$ 100.00	18 %	50 years	_____	_____

- *Introducing the % key*
- *Using the calculator effectively*
- *Building consumer awareness*

Name _____

3-3

The State's Little Bit Extra

Figuring sales tax

1. a. Assuming a sales tax of 7%, find the total cost for articles priced as follows:

Cost	Cost + Sales Tax
$ 7.00	_____
$12.00	_____
$ 8.00	_____
$ 2.00	_____
$ 4.70	_____
Total Bill	_____

b. Now find the total cost without any sales tax first. Then calculate the tax for that total amount.

c. Is the total bill any different? _____

d. This is an illustration of the distributive property. Explain. _____

2. a. Assuming a sales tax of 6%, find the total bill for a set of articles priced as follows:

Cost	Cost + Sales Tax
$ 5.00	_____
$ 4.80	_____
$ 2.44	_____
$ 7.30	_____
$ 5.60	_____
Total Bill	_____

b. Now use the calculator to find the total cost first and then add the sales tax.

c. Is there a difference? Explain. _____

d. Which method of calculating the total bill is fairer? Why?

_____

_____

_____

_____

_____

• *Using the % key*
• *Understanding taxation*

Advanced Calculator Math

3-4

Money, Money in the Bank: Part I

Understanding compound interest

1. Joan's grandfather gave her $100.00 to open a savings account.
At the end of each year, the bank pays 6% interest and adds it to the account.
Fill in the table to show how Joan's account increases.

Principal : $100   Interest Rate : 6%   Term : 5 years (compound interest)

	Principal $		Interest $		Total $
Year 1	100	+	$100 \times 0.06 = 6$	=	$100 + 6 = 106$
Year 2	106	+	6.36	=	112.36
Year 3	112.36	+		=	
Year 4		+		=	
Year 5		+		=	

Interest which is added to the account each year to form the principal
for the following year is called *compound interest*.
What is the difference between simple interest and compound interest?

_____

Which is more? _____ Why? _____

Which is fairer? _____

2. Fill in the table.

Principal : $100   Rate: 7%   Term : 6 years

	Principal $		Principal + Interest (Total) $
Year 1	100	`1 . 0 7 × 1 0 0` or `1 0 0 + 7 %`	107
Year 2	107		
Year 3	114.49		
Year 4			
Year 5			
Year 6			

• *Using the % key*
• *Understanding compound interest*
• *Using the calculator effectively*

Name _____

Advanced Calculator Math

3-5

Money, Money in the Bank: Part II

How compound interest adds up

1. Fill in the table.

Principal : $100   Rate of Interest : 8%   Loan Period : 5 years

Years	Principal + Interest Method A ([1] [0] [0] [+] [8] [%] [=] [=] [=] [=] [=])	Principal + Interest Method B [1] [0] [0] [×] [1] [.] [0] [8] [=] [=] [=] [=] [=]
1		
2		
3		
4		
5		

2. Discuss the differences between the two methods and answers.

_____

_____

3. Use the methods shown above to fill in this table.

Principal	Rate	Period	Total (Simple Interest)	Total (Compound Interest)
$ 400	7%	2 years		
$ 960	12%	3 years		
$1435	15%	5 years		
$2869	18%	7 years		
$5000	10%	10 years		

4. The family Mark babysat for was so pleased with his work that they promised and paid him a 10% increase over the previous year's rate at each of his birthdays. Mark decided to make a career out of babysitting for this family. He sat for nieces and nephews, then for the children's children, and finally for great-grandchildren. He started at age 12 for $1.00 per hour. At age 85, he was still sitting for the same family. What was his hourly rate at that time? _____

• *Using the % key*
• *Understanding compound interest*

3-6

How Fast Can You Estimate?

Rounding helps you figure faster

Estimate by rounding each number to a multiple of 5 or 10 before adding or subtracting.

1.

18 + 5 + 13 − 23 + 2 + 7 − 11 =	
75 − 27 + 57 − 78 − 42 + 14 − 2 =	
24 − 37 + 2 + 19 − 13 + 86 + 61 =	
78 + 89 − 5 − 68 + 1 + 14 − 53 =	
82 − 68 + 7 + 6 − 8 + 24 + 4 =	

2.

267 + 691 − 52 − 152 + 311 − 8 − 86 =	
49 + 308 + 89 − 81 − 59 + 631 − 90 =	
82 − 72 + 129 + 516 − 78 − 558 + 29 =	
951 − 926 + 82 + 54 − 16 − 27 − 19 =	
56 + 76 + 59 − 65 − 3 − 22 + 98 =	

3.

389 + 93 − 652 + 218 − 62 =	
96 + 21 − 126 − 235 + 540 =	
12 − 71 + 825 − 54 − 77 =	
232 − 26 + 323 − 983 + 230 =	
324 − 790 + 3 + 913 − 894 =	

Check your estimates with a calculator.
Put a check mark beside any estimate that is within 50 of the exact answer.
Put a star beside any estimate that is within 10 of the exact answer.

• *Reviewing estimation and rounding*
• *Rounding to the nearest five or ten*
• *Estimating positive and negative integers*

Name _____

Advanced Calculator Math

Copyright © 1980 by Fearon Pitman Publishers, Inc.

3-7

Smaller, Smaller, Smaller

Which triangles will vanish?

The "Bermuda Triangle" is a mysterious section of the Caribbean Ocean near Bermuda. It is said that many ships and airplanes have traveled into the area, and have never been heard from again.

Below is a collection of triangles, some of which are "Bermuda" triangles.

A triangle is a "Bermuda" triangle if, when you go around and around it, multiplying the numbers together, the product (answer) gets smaller and smaller, and seems to disappear (it approaches zero).

Put an X on the triangles which you estimate are "Bermuda" triangles.

Check your answers with your calculator.

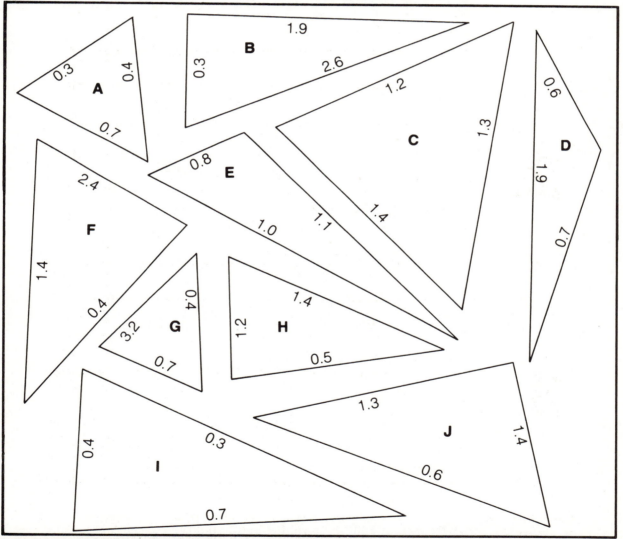

• *Estimating in multiplication*
• *Developing the concept of limits*

Name _____ *17*

3-8

All-Star Estimating

Think about the decimals first

Estimate each product to at least 2 significant digits.

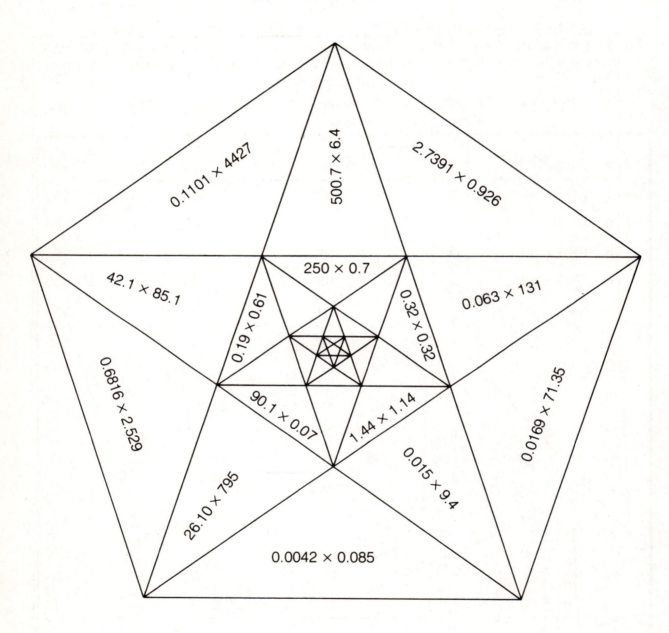

Check your estimates with your calculator.

- *Rounding with decimals*
- *Estimating in multiplication*

Advanced Calculator Math

3-9

Divide and Figure

Will rounding help you?

Circle the answer which is the best estimate for each quotient.
The first one is done for you.

1.

a. 2822 ÷ 24	(100)	150	200
b. 1632 ÷ 47	40	70	100
c. 7965 ÷ 94	60	80	100
d. 1338 ÷ 82	10	15	20
e. 2248 ÷ 73	10	20	30

2.

f. 3777 ÷ 15	150	200	250
g. 6345 ÷ 62	50	100	150
h. 1066 ÷ 95	10	20	50
i. 2790 ÷ 98	10	30	50
j. 4008 ÷ 86	10	30	50

3.

k. 5054 ÷ 53	50	100	150
l. 8492 ÷ 21	200	300	400
m. 1426 ÷ 69	10	20	30
n. 2396 ÷ 84	10	20	30
o. 4026 ÷ 69	40	60	80

4.

p. 8425 ÷ 54	100	150	200
q. 1336 ÷ 35	40	60	80
r. 1909 ÷ 90	10	15	20
s. 7439 ÷ 32	200	300	400
t. 5388 ÷ 93	50	75	100

Check your estimates with the calculator.

• *Reviewing estimation in division*
• *Rounding in division*

Name _____ *19*

3-10

Factor Finesse

Multiply accurately and win! (for 2 players)

Advanced Calculator Math

Equipment

Calculator   Spinner (below)   Score sheet, pencil   Thumbtack, short pencil

Instructions

1. Complete the spinner by pushing a thumbtack through the center from the back. Use a short pencil for a dial.

2. Player A displays a 2-digit number on the calculator (**for example, 59**).

3. Player B spins the dial to find the "factor" (**say, 11**). B must then change the display into a multiple of the number spun by adding or subtracting a 1-digit number (**say, 59 − 4 = 55**).

4. If the display is already a required multiple, players may say "Pass."

5. Player A may challenge B by checking on the calculator whether the display is indeed one of the required multiples. If it is not, the challenger (A) gains a point; otherwise the opponent (B) scores.

6. After each challenge, a new round starts. The winner is the player with the highest score after 10 rounds.

Variations

1. Start each round with a three-digit number in the display.

2. Use a spinner with large numbers on it.

3. Restrict the players to adding or subtracting a number adjacent (on the calculator) to the number that was spun. (**If, say, 57 was in the display and B spun 6, then B has to choose among ⟨2⟩ ⟨3⟩ ⟨5⟩ ⟨8⟩ ⟨9⟩ .**) There is no restriction if 10, 11, or 12 is spun.

Note that in this last variation there is no solution for numbers such as 65 and 70 if the call is for a multiple of 9. (No solution exists for numbers equivalent to 2 or 7 modulo 9.)

Round	Winner
1	
2	
3	
4	
5	
6	
7	
8	
9	
10	

7	8	9
4	5	6
1	2	3

- *Practicing multiplication and division facts*
- *Factoring*

Name _____

3-11

Name Your Numbers

Mental multiplication/division with care   (for 2 players)

Equipment
Calculator
2 score sheets, pencils

Instructions

1. Player A selects a number **(say, 500)** as the destination. Both players write it on their score sheets.

2. Player B announces the starting number **(say, 13).** Both players record this number, also.

3. Each player now writes down a "multiplier" (a number to multiply by 13 to get 500). Decimals are permitted.

4. The player whose product is closer to 500 wins the round. (Check with the calculator.) The winner puts a check mark in the ✔ column of his or her score sheet.

5. After each round, a new destination and a new starting number are chosen.

6. The player who wins the most rounds out of 10 is the champion.

Player A: _____					Player B: _____				
Destination	**Starting Number**	**Multiplier**	**Product**	✔	**Destination**	**Starting Number**	**Multiplier**	**Product**	✔
a					a				
b					b				
c					c				
d					d				
e					e				
f					f				
g					g				
h					h				
i					i				
j					j				

• *Practicing estimation with multiplication and division facts*

Advanced Calculator Math

Name _____

3-12

The "Get Mean" Game

Is it harder with more players?   (for 3 to 20 players)

Advanced Calculator Math

Equipment
Calculator (display covered)
Score sheet, pencil

Instructions

1. Each player estimates the average **weight**, age, allowance, height, or some other statistic, for the group of players, and writes down the guess.

2. Player A enters his or her own **weight**, age, allowance, or height, into the calculator.

3. Each player in turn adds his or her own figure.

4. Player A then divides the total by the number of players to find the mean, but does not announce it.

5. Each player announces his or her estimate.

6. "A" declares the winner.

7. In case of a tie, both players may be given a chance to revise their estimates.

	Score Sheet	
Statistic	**Mean**	**Winner**
Weight		
Age		
Allowance		
Height		
Waist		
Shoe Size		
Number in Family		

Copyright © 1980 by Fearon Pitman Publishers, Inc.

• *Collecting data*
• *Estimating an average*

Name _____

3-13

Right On!

Add on too much and you lose   (for 2 players)

Equipment

Calculator   Spinner (below)   Thumbtack
Paper and pencil   Short pencil

Instructions

1. Complete the spinner by pushing a thumbtack through the center from the back. Use a short pencil for a dial.

2. Player A selects a number such as 500 as the target and writes it down.

3. Player B spins the dial to get the starting number (say, 13), and stores it in the calculator as a multiplicative constant.
   (Press: ⊡ ⊡ ⊠ ⊟ . DON'T CLEAR!)

4. Player A attempts to multiply the starting number by a decimal number (say, 38.1) so that the result is 500.

5. Player B modifies A's choice to get even closer to the target. (say, 38.2)

6. Player A modifies B's choice, and so on. (38.4, 38.41, . . .)

7. The first player to get the calculator to show the target in the display is the winner.

8. Anyone who goes over the target loses.

9. Play a "best-of-7" series.

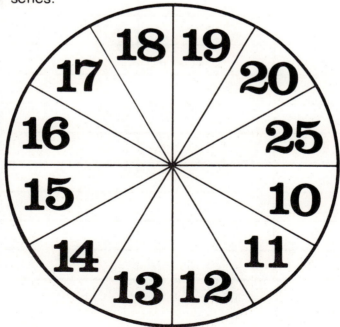

• *Estimating a factor with precision*
• *Multiplying with decimal fractions*

Name _____ 23

3-14

Pretty Square

Guessing square roots to win   (for 2 players)

Equipment
Calculator
Score sheet, pencil

Instructions

1. While Player B looks away, Player A picks 4 consecutive numbers, multiplies them together, and adds 1. A then writes down this "target" number and shows it to B.
2. Player B has one try to estimate the square root of the target.
3. If B is wrong, A takes a turn.
4. Players continue taking turns until one player finds the correct square root.
5. The player who finds the square root scores a point. Mark the winner on the score sheet (below).
6. Players take turns starting new rounds by constructing the target number.
7. The winner of the most rounds wins the match.

Round	Target	Winner (A or B)
1		
2		
3		
4		
5		
6		
7		
8		
9		
10		

Advanced Calculator Math

Copyright © 1980 by Fearon Pitman Publishers, Inc.

• *Estimating in multiplication and division*
• *Finding square roots*

Name _____

3-15

Animal, Vegetable, or Numeral?

Twenty Questions for math   (for 3 to 5 players)

Equipment
1 calculator per person   Paper and pencil

Instructions
1. Appoint one person as the Game Leader (G.L.).
2. G.L. writes down a 1-, 2-, or 3-digit number on a piece of paper.
3. Player A tries to find the number by asking questions that G.L. can answer with "Yes" or "No."
4. Whenever G.L. answers "No," it is the next player's turn to ask questions. A player who believes he or she knows the answer waits until his or her turn and then asks, "Is it 297?" (or whatever the guess may be).
5. The player who guesses the hidden number correctly, wins.
6. The person to the left of the G.L. is the Game Leader for the next round.
7. Players may use their calculators to help prepare questions. The Game Leader may use a calculator to help supply answers.

Example:
Mary is game leader for the first game. She writes 324 on a piece of paper.

		Mary:	
Penny:	Is the number 2 or more digits long?	Yes	
	Is it 2 digits long?	No	
Jim:	Is it 3 digits long?	Yes	
	Is it divisible by 2?	Yes	
	Is it divisible by 3?	Yes	
	Is it divisible by 4?	Yes	
	Is it divisible by 5?	No	
Dale:	Is it the number 756?	No	
Kate:	Is it bigger than 200?	Yes	
	Is it bigger than 500?	No	
Penny:	Is it more than 300?	Yes	
	Is it more than 400?	No	
Jim:	Is the sum of the digits less than 10?	Yes	
	Is the sum of the digits 9?	Yes	
	Is the number 324?	Yes	Jim wins!

• *Gathering data*
• *Using factors and multiples*
• *Developing problem-solving strategies*

Name _____ 25

3-16

A Decimal by Another Name

Converting decimals to fractions

Advanced Calculator Math

If you were to divide 312 by 4 and multiply your answer by 4 again,
what do you think your answer would be? _____
Try it on your calculator.

If you were to divide any counting number by 4 and multiply your
answer by 4 again, what do you think your answer would be? _____
Try it on your calculator. Write down 5 examples.

a. _____ **b.** _____ **c.** _____ **d.** _____ **e.** _____

A number is divided by 4. The answer is 1.25. What was the original number? _____

A number is divided by 8. The result is 0.375. What was the original number? _____

0.375 equals what fraction? _____

A number is divided by 25. The result is 0.92. What was the number that was divided by 25?
_____

The decimal fraction $0.92 = \dfrac{}{25}$.

Change the following decimal fractions to fractions with the required denominator

$0.3 = \dfrac{}{10}$ $0.4 = \dfrac{}{5}$ $0.75 = \dfrac{}{4}$ $0.3125 = \dfrac{}{16}$ $0.625 = \dfrac{}{8}$

$0.095 = \dfrac{}{200}$ $0.6 = \dfrac{}{15}$ $0.064 = \dfrac{}{125}$ $0.2125 = \dfrac{}{80}$ $0.75 = \dfrac{}{32}$

From the problems, you can show that $\dfrac{3}{4} = \dfrac{24}{32}$. How?

_____

Without using the table, you might still change $\dfrac{3}{4}$ to $\dfrac{24}{32}$ by thinking

$$\frac{3}{4} = 0.75 = \frac{?}{32}.$$

_____

• *Converting decimals to fractions*
• *Working with equivalent fractions*

Name _____

Copyright © 1980 by Fearon Pitman Publishers, Inc.

3-17

It's All Equal

No-sweat fraction alterations

Use your calculator to change $\frac{3}{5}$ to another fraction with denominator 25.

The answer should be $\frac{3}{5} = \frac{15}{25}$.

Similarly, change the following fractions to equivalent forms.

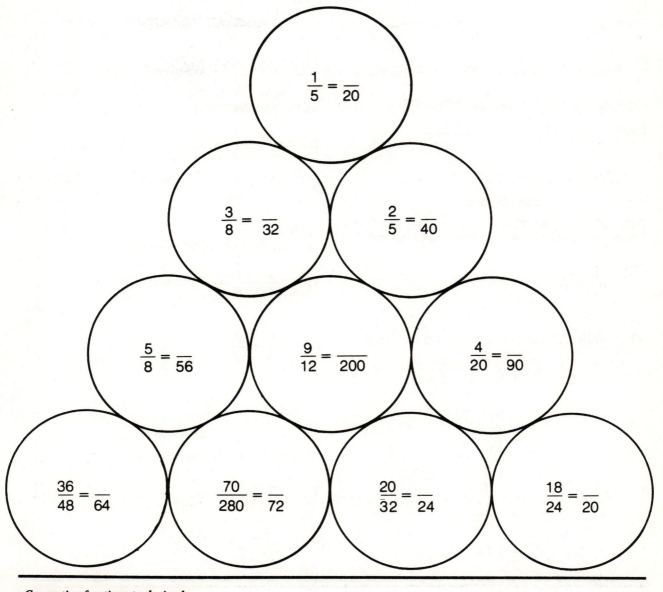

$\frac{1}{5} = \frac{}{20}$

$\frac{3}{8} = \frac{}{32}$

$\frac{2}{5} = \frac{}{40}$

$\frac{5}{8} = \frac{}{56}$

$\frac{9}{12} = \frac{}{200}$

$\frac{4}{20} = \frac{}{90}$

$\frac{36}{48} = \frac{}{64}$

$\frac{70}{280} = \frac{}{72}$

$\frac{20}{32} = \frac{}{24}$

$\frac{18}{24} = \frac{}{20}$

• *Converting fractions to decimals*
• *Working with equivalent fractions*

Name _____

3-18

The Calculating Fraction: Part I

How a calculator handles fractions

Most calculators are not capable of showing common fractions on their displays. Therefore, common fractions are usually changed to decimals for calculators.

Advanced Calculator Math

Exercise A

Change to decimal fractions. (You may use your calculator if don't remember these yet.)

$\dfrac{1}{2} =$ _____ $\dfrac{5}{8} =$ _____

$\dfrac{3}{4} =$ _____

How would you compute the decimal fraction for $\dfrac{27}{45}$? _____

Exercise B

Add, showing all work.
Change your answer to a decimal fraction.

$\dfrac{2}{5} + \dfrac{3}{4} =$ _____

Your work should look something like this:

$$\frac{2}{5} + \frac{3}{4} = \frac{2 \times 4}{5 \times 4} + \frac{3 \times 5}{4 \times 5}$$

$$= \frac{8}{20} + \frac{15}{20}$$

$$= \frac{23}{20}$$

$$= 1\frac{3}{20}$$

$$= 1\frac{15}{100}$$

$$= 1.15$$

It would be easy to change each fraction to a decimal first, and then add. For example:

$$\frac{2}{5} + \frac{3}{4} = 0.4 + 0.75 \qquad \begin{array}{r} 0.4 \\ 0.75 \\ \hline 1.15 \end{array}$$

$$= 1.15$$

Exercise C

Try these. (Write the intermediate steps, as in the example.)

1. $\dfrac{3}{4} + \dfrac{7}{8} =$ _____

2. $\dfrac{1}{2} + \dfrac{7}{16} =$ _____

Your work should look like this:

1. $\dfrac{3}{4} + \dfrac{7}{8} = 0.75 + 0.875$
   $= 1.625$

2. $\dfrac{1}{2} + \dfrac{7}{16} = 0.5 + 0.4375$
   $= 0.9375$

Exercise D

Now try these. Show your work.

1. $\dfrac{9}{25} + \dfrac{36}{64} =$

2. $\dfrac{15}{24} + \dfrac{35}{40} =$

• *Adding and subtracting common fractions*
• *Using the calculator optimally*
• *Working with the distributive property*
28 • *Working with calculator algorithms*

Copyright © 1980 by Fearon Pitman Publishers, Inc.

Name _____

3-19

The Calculating Fraction: Part II

More on how the calculator handles fractions

1. Addition

Try $\frac{1}{2} + \frac{7}{16} =$

You should have punched in $\boxed{1}\ \boxed{\div}\ \boxed{2}\ \boxed{\times}\ \boxed{1}\ \boxed{6}\ \boxed{+}\ \boxed{7}\ \boxed{\div}\ \boxed{1}\ \boxed{6}$

Correct answer: 0.9375

Exercise A

1. $\frac{5}{8} + \frac{1}{4} =$ 　　2. $\frac{17}{20} + \frac{4}{5} =$ 　　3. $\frac{6}{10} + \frac{19}{40} =$ 　　4. $\frac{5}{16} + \frac{1}{2} =$

Answers: 1. 0.875　2. 1.65　3. 1.075　4. 0.8125

2. Subtraction

Example: $\frac{3}{4} - \frac{1}{2} =$ $\boxed{3}\ \boxed{\div}\ \boxed{4}\ \boxed{\times}\ \boxed{2}\ \boxed{-}\ \boxed{1}\ \boxed{\div}\ \boxed{2}$ = 0.25

Exercise B

1. $\frac{5}{8} - \frac{3}{10} =$ 　　2. $\frac{15}{16} - \frac{3}{4} =$ 　　3. $\frac{7}{8} - \frac{13}{40} =$ 　　4. $\frac{9}{16} - \frac{1}{2} =$

Answers: 1. 0.325　2. 0.1875　3. 0.55　4. 0.0625

3. Chain Additions

Examples:

1. $\frac{3}{4} + \frac{1}{2} + 6$

$\boxed{3}\ \boxed{\div}\ \boxed{4}\ \boxed{\times}\ \boxed{2}\ \boxed{+}\ \boxed{1}\ \boxed{\div}\ \boxed{2}\ \boxed{+}\ \boxed{6}$ = 7.25

2. $\frac{3}{4} + \frac{1}{2} + \frac{5}{8}$

$\boxed{3}\ \boxed{\div}\ \boxed{4}\ \boxed{\times}\ \boxed{2}\ \boxed{+}\ \boxed{1}\ \boxed{\div}\ \boxed{2}\ \boxed{\times}\ \boxed{8}\ \boxed{+}\ \boxed{5}\ \boxed{\div}\ \boxed{8}$ = 1.875

Exercise C

1. $\frac{3}{4} + \frac{7}{16} + \frac{11}{40} =$ 　　2. $\frac{1}{10} + \frac{7}{8} + \frac{5}{16} =$ 　　3. $\frac{3}{8} + \frac{2}{5} - \frac{1}{2} =$ 　　4. $\frac{6}{8} - \frac{1}{16} - \frac{3}{20} =$

Answers: 1. 1.4625　2. 1.2875　3. 0.275　4. 0.5375

• *Adding and subtracting common fractions*
• *Using the calculator optimally*
• *Working with the distributive property*
• *Working with calculator algorithms*

Name _____

3-20

Fast Fractions

How you help your calculator do it

Exercise A

1. $\dfrac{3}{7} \times 4 =$

2. $\dfrac{2}{5} \times 12 =$

3. $5 \times \dfrac{2}{9} =$

4. $8 \times \dfrac{4}{3} =$

Answers: 1. 1.7142857 2. 4.8 3. 1.1111111 4. 10.666666

Find a way to do $\dfrac{7}{10} \times \dfrac{5}{8}$ on your machine. Your answer should be 0.4375.

One way is
$\boxed{}$ × $\boxed{}$ ÷ $\boxed{}$ ÷ $\boxed{}$

Exercise B

1. $\dfrac{5}{6} \times \dfrac{9}{10} =$

2. $\dfrac{3}{4} \times \dfrac{5}{8} =$

3. $\dfrac{3}{8} \times \dfrac{7}{5} =$

4. $\dfrac{4}{14} \times \dfrac{7}{4} =$

5. $\dfrac{13}{29} \times \dfrac{5}{26} =$

Answers: 1. 0.75 2. 0.46875 3. 0.525 4. 0.5 5. 0.0862068

Exercise C

1. $\dfrac{5}{8} \times \dfrac{4}{6} \times \dfrac{9}{10} =$

2. $\dfrac{7}{16} \times \dfrac{2}{5} \times \dfrac{5}{12} =$

3. $\dfrac{5}{6} \times \dfrac{5}{8} \times \dfrac{33}{8} =$

4. $\dfrac{4}{15} \times \dfrac{5}{26} \times \dfrac{100}{3} =$

Answers: 1. 0.375 2. 0.0729166 3. 2.1484375 4. 1.7094016

- *Using the calculator optimally*
- *Multiplying fractions*
- *Working with calculator algorithms*

Name _____

Advanced Calculator Math

3-21

Be a Number Detective: Part I

Can you predict the patterns?

Advanced Calculator Math

1. Use your calculator:

1 ÷ 3 = _____

10 ÷ 33 = _____

100 ÷ 333 = _____

Predict:

1000 ÷ _____ = _____

10,000 ÷ _____ = _____

100,000 ÷ _____ = _____

Check your guesses.

2. Use your calculator:

1 ÷ 7 = _____

2 ÷ 7 = _____

3 ÷ 7 = _____

Predict:

4 ÷ 7 = _____

____ ÷ 7 = _____

____ ÷ ____ = _____

Hint: look at the order of the digits.

3. Use your calculator:

1 × 9 = _____

11 × 99 = _____

111 × 999 = _____

1111 × 9999 = _____

Predict:

11,111 × 99,999 = _____

111,111 × 999,999 = _____

• *Detecting and completing patterns*

Name _____

3-22

Be a Number Detective: Part II
More patterns to figure out

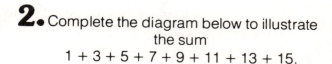

1	=	1	=	1^2	
1 + 3	=	4	=	2^2	
1 + 3 + 5	=	_____	=	_____	
1 + 3 + 5 + 7	=	_____	=	_____	
1 + 3 + 5 + 7 + 9	=	_____	=	_____	
1 + 3 + 5 + 7 + 9 + 11	=	_____	=	_____	
1 + 3 + 5 + 7 + 9 + 11 + 13	=	_____	=	_____	
Guess: 1 + 3 + 5 + . . . + 19	=	_____	=	_____	

1. To understand what is happening, count the number of dots in each section of the square.

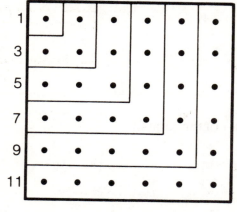

However, the whole figure is a square containing 6 × 6 dots.

Therefore, $1 + 3 + 5 + 7 + 9 + 11 = 6^2$.

2. Complete the diagram below to illustrate the sum

1 + 3 + 5 + 7 + 9 + 11 + 13 + 15.

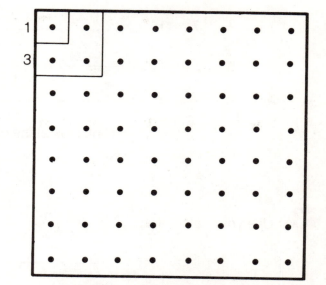

Write the corresponding number sentence.

Use your calculator to check whether 1 + 3 + 5 + 7 + . . . + 31 is a perfect square.

• *Detecting and completing patterns*
• *Explaining patterns*
• *Squaring and square root*

Name _____

Advanced Calculator Math

Copyright © 1980 by Fearon Pitman Publishers, Inc.

3-23

Be a Square Detective

Showing squares with dot patterns

1	=	1	=	1^2
1 + 2 + 1	=	4	=	2^2
1 + 2 + 3 + 2 + 1	= _____	= _____
1 + 2 + 3 + 4 + 3 + 2 + 1	= _____	= _____
1 + 2 + 3 + 4 + 5 + 4 + 3 + 2 + 1	= _____	= _____
__ + __ + __ + __ + __ + __ + __ + __ + __ + __	= _____	= _____

Now guess:

1 + 2 + 3 + 4 + 5 + 6 + 7 + 8 + 9 + 10 + 9 + 8 + 7 + 6 + 5 + 4 + 3 + 2 + 1 = _____

= _____

1. Use this dot pattern to explain what is happening.

———————————————→ 1

———————————————→ 2

———————————————→

———————————————→

———————————————→

———————————————→

———————————————→

Total _____

But the whole figure is a square containing _____ × _____ dots.

Therefore, 1 + 2 + 3 + 4 + 3 + 2 + 1 = (_____)².

2. Draw a similar dot diagram to explain why
1 + 2 + 3 + 4 + 5 + 4 + 3 + 2 + 1 = 5².

• *Detecting and explaining patterns*
• *Squaring and square root*

Name_____33

3-24

The Three-Angle Detective

Dot patterns for triangles

$$
\begin{array}{rcl}
1 & = & 1 \\
1+2 & = & 3 \\
1+2+3 & = & 6 \\
1+2+3+4 & = & \rule{3cm}{0.4pt} \\
1+2+3+4+5 & = & \rule{3cm}{0.4pt} \\
1+2+3+4+5+6 & = & \rule{3cm}{0.4pt} \\
1+2+3+4+5+6+7 & = & \rule{3cm}{0.4pt}
\end{array}
$$

$$= \quad 4 \quad = \quad 2^2$$
$$= \quad 9 \quad = \quad \underline{}^2$$
$$= \quad \underline{} \quad = \quad \underline{}^2$$
$$= \quad \underline{} \quad = \quad \underline{}$$
$$= \quad \underline{} \quad = \quad \underline{}$$
$$= \quad \underline{} \quad = \quad \underline{}$$

The numbers 1, 3, 6, 10, etc., are called triangular numbers.
Look at the dot pattern to see why.

What seems to happen when one triangular number is added to the next one?

_____

Explain, using the dot pattern below.

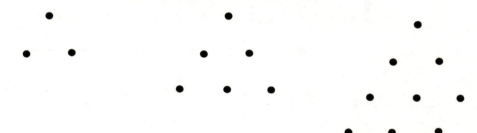

_____

_____

• *Detecting and completing patterns*
• *Explaining patterns*
• *Squaring and square root*

Name _____

Advanced Calculator Math

Copyright © 1980 by Fearon Pitman Publishers, Inc.

3-25

Pattern Power

Can you explain these patterns?

1.
6 × 9 = _____
6 × 99 = _____
6 × 999 = _____
6 × _____ = _____
___ × _____ = _____
___ × _____ = _____

2.
9 × 6 = _____
9 × 66 = _____
9 × 666 = _____
9 × _____ = _____
___ × _____ = _____
___ × _____ = _____

Compare your answers for 1 and 2. Explain:

_____

_____

_____

3.
4 × 2 = _____
4 × 22 = _____
4 × 222 = _____
4 × _____ = _____
___ × _____ = _____
___ × _____ = _____

4.
2 × 4 = _____
2 × 44 = _____
2 × 444 = _____
2 × _____ = _____
___ × _____ = _____
___ × _____ = _____

Compare your answers for 3 and 4. Explain:

_____

_____

_____

5. Pick any two 1-digit numbers **(say, 3 and 8)**. Form a pattern like those on this page.

$$3 \times 8 = \qquad 8 \times 3 =$$
$$3 \times 88 = \qquad 8 \times 33 =$$
$$\vdots \qquad\qquad \vdots$$

Compare the answers. Explain. Try another example.

• *Detecting patterns*
• *Explaining patterns*
• *Understanding number properties*
• *Developing algebraic reasoning*

Name _____

3-26

More Pattern Power

More exploration of patterns

1. Store any 1-digit number in your calculator.

Multiply by 3. Multiply by 37.

Compare your answer with the original number. Explain:

_____

_____

_____

2. Store any 1-digit number in your calculator.

Multiply by 13. Multiply by 7. Multiply by 11. Multiply by 37. Multiply by 3.

Compare your answer with the starting number. Explain:

_____

_____

_____

_____

3. Store any 3-digit number in your calculator.

Multiply by 13. Multiply by 7. Multiply by 11.

Compare your answer with your starting number. Explain:

_____

_____

_____

4. Store any 1-digit number in your calculator.

Multiply by 16. Multiply by 43. Multiply by 1483.

Look for the pattern in your answer. Explain:

_____

_____

_____

- *Detecting patterns*
- *Explaining patterns*
- *Understanding number properties*
- *Developing algebraic reasoning*

Name _____

Advanced Calculator Math

Copyright © 1980 by Fearon Pitman Publishers, Inc.

3-27

Super Pattern Power

See if you can explain these

Advanced Calculator Math

1.

$1 \times 7 \times 11 \times 13 =$ _____

$2 \times 7 \times 11 \times 13 =$ _____

$3 \times 7 \times 11 \times 13 =$ _____

$4 \times 7 \times 11 \times 13 =$ _____

Explain: _____

_____

_____

2.

$1 \div 11 =$ _____

$2 \div 11 =$ _____

$3 \div 11 =$ _____

$4 \div 11 =$ _____

___ $\div$ ___ $=$ _____

___ $\div$ ___ $=$ _____

Explain: _____

_____

_____

3.

$12{,}345{,}679 \times \quad 9 =$ _____

$12{,}345{,}679 \times \quad 18 =$ _____

$12{,}345{,}679 \times \quad 27 =$ _____

$12{,}345{,}679 \times$ ___ $=$ _____

_____ $\times$ ___ $=$ _____

_____ $\times$ ___ $=$ _____

Explain: _____

_____

_____

4.

$2 + 4 \qquad = \quad 6 = 2 \times 3$

$2 + 4 + 6 \qquad = \quad 12 = 3 \times 4$

$2 + 4 + 6 + 8 \qquad =$ ___ $=$ _____

$2 + 4 + 6 + 8 + 10 =$ ___ $=$ _____

Use the array of blocks to explain why
$2 + 4 + 6 + 8 + 10 = 5 \times 6$.

_____

_____

_____

_____

_____

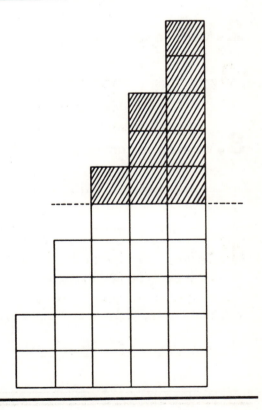

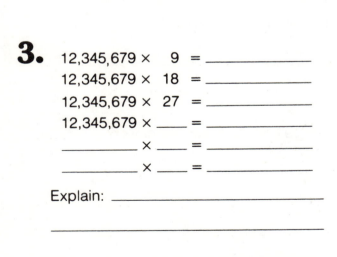

- *Detecting patterns*
- *Explaining patterns*
- *Understanding number properties*
- *Developing algebraic reasoning*

Name _____

3-28

Just a Little Bit Closer

What is a convergent sequence?

1. Use your calculator to find the decimal equivalents of the following:

Write the next 3 numbers and their decimal equivalents.

a. $\dfrac{1}{2} =$

b. $\dfrac{2}{3} =$

c. $\dfrac{3}{4} =$

d. $\dfrac{4}{5} =$

e. $\dfrac{5}{6} =$

f. $\dfrac{6}{7} =$

g. $\dfrac{7}{8} =$

h.

i.

j.

2. Mark the values on the number line.

```
├────────┼─────────────────────┼─────────────────────┤
0                               1                     1
                                ─
                                2
```

3. What do you notice when each term is compared to the next one?

_____

_____

4. To what number are the terms of the sequence getting closer and closer? _____ How can you test that guess?

_____

_____

_____

• *Detecting patterns*
• *Conceptualizing limits*

Name _____

Advanced Calculator Math

Copyright © 1980 by Fearon Pitman Publishers, Inc.

3-29

How Close Can You Get?

More about convergent sequences

Here is another sequence: $\dfrac{2}{1}, \dfrac{3}{2}, \dfrac{4}{3}, \dfrac{5}{4}, \cdots$

1. Again, use your calculator to find the decimal equivalents of these terms:

a. $\dfrac{2}{1} =$

b. $\dfrac{3}{2} =$

c. $\dfrac{4}{3} =$

d. $\dfrac{5}{4} =$

e. $\dfrac{6}{5} =$

f. $\dfrac{7}{6} =$

g. $\dfrac{8}{7} =$

Find the next 3 terms in the sequence and the decimal equivalents.

h.

i.

j.

2. Mark each term on the number line.

```
  |                             |                             |
  1                           1 1/2                           2
```

3. What do you notice when each term in the sequence is compared to the next one?

_____

4. What number is the sequence getting closer and closer to? _____
That number is called the limit of that sequence.

5. Can you think of a sequence which has a limit of 0? Check your guess with the calculator. What is the sequence?

_____

6. Can you find a sequence which has a limit of $\dfrac{1}{2}$? Hint: The denominator may have to be at least twice as large as the numerator. (There are other ways, also.) Check with your calculator. What is the sequence?

_____

• *Detecting patterns*
• *Conceptualizing limits*
• *Understanding convergent sequence*

Advanced Calculator Math

Name _____ 39

3-30

Paper Folding Challenge

Creases, pieces, lines, and numbers

1. A point divides a line into two parts.

Two points divide a line into how many parts?

Fill in the table to show points and parts.

Number of Points	Number of Parts
1	2
2	
3	
4	
6	
82	

2. Fold a sheet of paper in half. Fold the paper again in the same direction as before (see the illustration). Into how many parts is the paper divided? Complete the table.

Number of Times Folded	Number of Parts	Number of Creases
1	2	1
2	4	3
3		
4		
5		
10		
20		

3. Fold a sheet of paper in half. Fold again in the other direction. Into how many parts is the paper divided? How many crease lines go all the way across the page?

Number of Times Folded	Number of Parts	Number of Crease Lines
1	2	1
2		
3		
4		
5		
6		
20		

• *Detecting patterns*
• *Developing mathematical reasoning*

Name _____

Advanced Calculator Math

3-31

The New You

The price of a shopping spree

Get a department store catalog.
Buy yourself a complete set of clothes.
Make a list of your purchases, the cost of each item, and the total cost.
Don't forget the sales tax!

• *Gathering data*
• *Constructing tables*
• *Computing tax*

Name _____

3-32

Best Buys

Who's the smartest shopper?

Circle the "best buys" for each item.

Item	Brand A		Brand B	
	Size	**Cost**	**Size**	**Cost**
Chips	50 g	20¢	40 g	19¢
Onions	1 kg	39¢	1.5 kg	50¢
Pickles	750 mL	2 for $1.49	800 mL	3 for $2.09
Hamburger	800 g	$1.47	900 g	$1.60
Cheese	0.5 kg pack	2 packs for $1.49	0.75 kg pack	$1.07
Apples	10	98¢ a doz.	10	2 for 19¢
Jelly	50 mL	3 for 89¢	25 mL	7 for $1
Pop	300 mL	6 for $1.49	750 mL	$0.33 ea
Bread	500 g	3 for $1.45	750 g	2 for $1.45
Soap	100 g	2 for 63¢	150 g	3 for 99¢

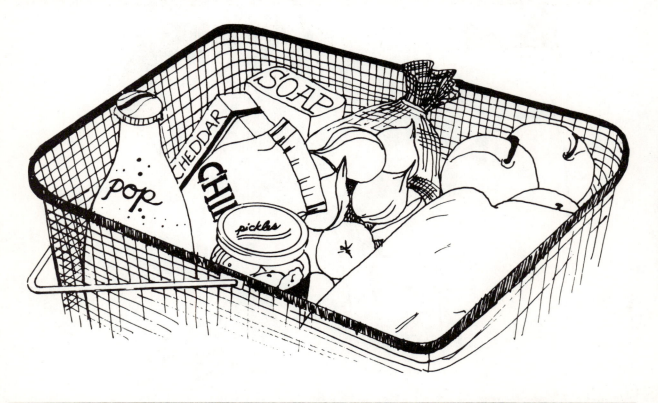

Advanced Calculator Math

Copyright © 1980 by Fearon Pitman Publishers, Inc.

• *Working with ratio*
• *Building consumer awareness*
• *Using the calculator judiciously*

Name _____

3-33

Batter Up!

What are their batting averages?

Fill in the table.
(The calculations for the first line are shown below the table.)

Name	Hits	Times at Bat	Batting Average
Jones	84	304	0.276
Berstein	95	310	
Duncan	83	340	
Washington	96	295	
Kew	26	141	
Park	37	162	
Brown	121	351	
Kolinski	134	400	
Sauvé	85	304	
Totals			**Team Average**

Jones' Batting Average	=	Hits ÷ Times at Bat
	=	84 ÷ 304
	=	0.2763157
	=	0.276

1. Which player would be the best one to have on your team? Explain your choice.

2. Can the team average be found in two ways? Explain.

Advanced Calculator Math

• *Finding and evaluating averages*
• *Discerning the basis for an average*

Name _____

3-34

If the Shoe Fits . . .

There's data all around you

1. Buy running shoes for your family.

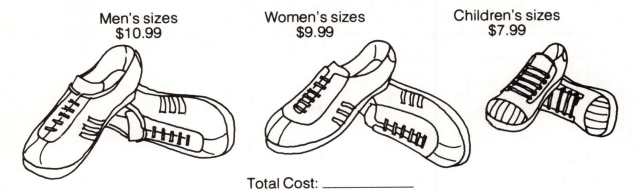

Men's sizes
$10.99

Women's sizes
$9.99

Children's sizes
$7.99

Total Cost: _____

2. Count the shoelace eyelets in your shoes.
Choose 5 friends and count their shoelace eyelets.
(Write "0" if someone wears shoes without eyelets.)

a. Fill in the table.

Name	Number of eyelets

b. Find the average number of eyelets per person in the group.

c. Use this average to get an estimate for the number of shoe eyelets in your class.

d. Use the average to estimate the number of shoe eyelets in the country, assuming that everyone owns 4 pairs of shoes.

e. Write down some of the assumptions you made to solve these problems.

• *Gathering data*
• *Finding averages*
• *Finding ratios*

Name _____

Advanced Calculator Math

3-35

Faster Than a Speeding Snail

Processing data with your calculator

This is a table of top running speeds of humans and various animals.

Animal	Speed (km/h)	Animal	Speed (km/h)
Pig	17.5	Greyhound	63
Quarter Horse	76.5	Gray fox	67.5
Rabbit	56	Grizzly Bear	48
Zebra	64	Human	45
Lion	80	Chicken	14.5
Garden Snail	0.05	Tortoise	0.27
Cheetah	112	Sloth	0.24

a. Arrange the animals in order of speed.

b. Find the ratios comparing the top speed of the animals with that of humans.

c. Put the result on the graph below.

**Ratio of Top Running Speed of Animals
to Top Running Speed of Humans**

• *Calculating ratios*
• *Constructing graphs*
• *Using constants*

Name _____

3-36

Pop Pop and Fizz Fizz

More data to collect and refine

1. Ask 5 friends to tell you how many bottles or cans (300 mL) of pop they drank each day during the last week.

Fill in the table. Calculate the totals.

Name	Day 1	Day 2	Day 3	Day 4	Day 5	Day 6	Day 7	Total
Total								

2. **a.** Calculate the average amount of pop you and your friends drank per day.

   b. At today's prices, how much would a year's supply of pop cost for you and your friends?

• *Gathering data*
• *Finding averages and ratios*
• *Building consumer awareness*

Name _____

Advanced Calculator Math

Copyright © 1980 by Fearon Pitman Publishers, Inc.

3-37

A Day in Your Life

Data on how people spend time

a. Estimate how many hours per Tuesday you spend at the following activities. Write your estimates in the first column.

Number of Hours								
Activity	**You**	**Friend A**	**Friend B**	**Friend C**	**Friend D**	**Friend E**	**Total**	**Average**
Sleeping								
Eating								
Playing								
Helping								
Watching Television								
Attending School								
Other								
Total	24 h							

b. Ask 5 of your classmates to fill in the next 5 columns.

c. Complete the table.

d. Using the average results, complete this table.

Activity	**Number of Minutes**	**Percentage of the Time**
Sleeping		
Eating		
Playing		
Helping		
Watching Television		
Attending School		
Other		
Total	1440 m	100%

• *Gathering data*
• *Finding averages*
• *Finding percentages*
• *Reading and constructing tables*

Name _____

Advanced Calculator Math

3-38

Kool-Punch and Cake

These problems are easy with the calculator

Advanced Calculator Math

1. Kool-Punch Stand

Bill's Kool-Punch stand was a gigantic success.

He sold $1.55 worth of drinks to 31 customers, and made a profit of 63¢.

a. What was the cost per glass? **b.** What is his profit per glass? **c.** What is the % mark-up?

Based on this success, Bill opened a nationwide chain of Kool-Punch stands (Bill's Kentucky-Frozen Kool-Punch). If everyone in the country bought 1 glass on a particularly hot day, what would Bill's profit be?

2. Largest Cake

The world's largest birthday cake weighed 11,365 kg.
Here is a standard cake recipe:

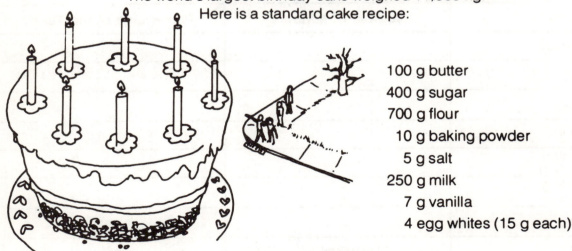

100 g butter

400 g sugar

700 g flour

10 g baking powder

5 g salt

250 g milk

7 g vanilla

4 egg whites (15 g each)

Rewrite the recipe so that it will make an 11,365 kg cake.

• *Finding ratios and percentages*
• *Working with metric quantities*

Name _____

3-39

Money Matters

A serious problem and two for fun

1. Up in Smoke

Find out the cost of a package of cigarettes. What would it cost to buy 1 pack daily for a year? For 40 years? (If the smoker lives that long!)

For x-perts:

Check with a person who smokes to find out how many packs per day he or she smokes. Compute his or her smoking cost per year.

2. Heavy Expenses

Find the mass of a

penny: _____ g

nickel: _____ g

dime: _____ g

quarter: _____ g

dollar bill: _____ g

Calculate the mass of $100 in

pennies: _____

nickels: _____

dimes: _____

quarters: _____

dollar bills: _____

3. Discount Babysitting

Bill's Baby Business announces a special for November. Babysitting rates are $1.00 per hour for the first child, half of that for the second child, half of the cost of the second child for the third child, and so on.

a. Find Bill's rate per hour for 2 children. _____

b. For 3 children. _____

c. For 6 children. _____

d. What is his maximum rate per hour? _____

Copyright © 1980 by Fearon Pitman Publishers, Inc.

Advanced Calculator Math

• *Collecting data*
• *Finding the mass of an object*
• *Conceptualizing a limit*
• *Finding rates*

Name _____

3-40

Round Things

Working with pi

Tire

Belted Safety 40,000 km Treadwear-Rated

Cost: $37.50   Diameter: 83 cm

Cost per kilometer = _____

Number of revolutions required to go 40,000 km = _____

Ferris Wheel Riding

The world record for ferris wheel riding is 21 d 3 h 58 min (i.e., 21 days, 3 hours, 58 minutes).
During that time, the rider traveled 1158.728 km (in circles) in 11,800 revolutions.

a. What was the diameter of the wheel?

b. How long did the wheel take to travel 1 revolution?

c. How long did the rider take to travel 1 km?

d. What was the speed of the wheel in revolutions per minute?

e. What was the speed of the rider in kilometers per hour?

• *Working with pi*
• *Working with ratios*
• *Finding rates of speed*

Name _____

Advanced Calculator Math

Copyright © 1980 by Fearon Pitman Publishers, Inc.

3-41

Moo!

Finding the larger facts

A certain hamburger chain claims to have sold 20,000,000,000 hamburgers.
The average hamburger has 100 g of meat, 2.5 mL of ketchup, and 0.3 g of salt.

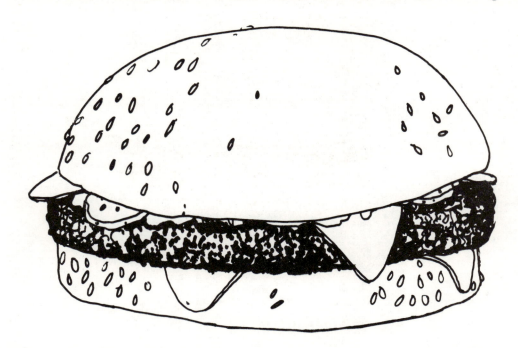

1. If a cow yields 150 kg of beef, how many cows were needed for these hamburgers?

2. How many tanker trucks, each holding 6 m³, would be needed to deliver the ketchup?

3. How many tons of salt were used?

For Experts

Make up your own problem about the pickles found in some hamburgers.
Solve your problem.

• *Working with large numbers*
• *Working with ratios*

3-42

From One Small Piece

It's easier than counting everything

---

201 OGALLALA DIRECTORY WES/ZIO

WESTERN OUTLOOK MAGAZINE
414 7th St E (Box 716) 284-2655
WESTERN OUTLOOK PUBLIC RELATIONS
414 7th St E (Box 716) 284-2655
WESTERN PARADISE MOTEL 221 1st St E 284-3684
WESTERN SCALE CO
123 10th St E PO Box 387 284-4636
Shop 284-6900
WESTFAHL Dick (Patricia) 915 E Street W 284-3166
WESTMORE Ervin C 120 7th St W 284-6873
WESTSIDE TEXACO
517 W 1st St. **284-6037**
WESTSIDE TIRE & MUFFLER 517 1st St W 284-6037
WHALEN James R Father 417 3rd St E 284-3196
WHEELER James A (Kay) 519 Platteview Dr 284-3026
WHEELER John Sunset Haven (G) 352-4459
WHEELER Robert (L) 355-2416
WHEELERS Highway 30W 284-3962
WHIPPLE Kim Fosters Trlr Ct (G) 352-2194
WHIPS Fletcher (G) 352-4096
WHIPS Jennie 504 Garfield Av (G) 352-4607
WHIPS Jerry (G) 352-4085
WHITE Delma 624 K Street W 284-2827
WHITE Lloyd E (Donita) (Box 366) (LM) 284-6518
WHITE Walter 621 Central Av (G) 352-4855
WHITEHURST James W 101 Skyline Dr 284-6982
WHITELEY Roy D (Ronnie) 1335 8th St E 284-3059
WHITMAN Mildred 821 Logan (G) 352-2160
WHITWER Clint 345 Garfield Av (G) 352-2167
WID Elmer 821 Logan (G) 352-4585
WID Erik (Uda) 712 F Street W 284-4827
WIDENER Melvin (Hilda) 406 3rd St W 284-3889
WIDFELDT Helmer M (Alta) 1520 6th St E 284-3389
WIEBE Carl (LM) 284-2513
WIECHMANN Don (Karen) (B Sp) 889-3352
WIENS Esther 537 Warren Av (G) 352-4541
WIEST Arvid D (Althea) (B) 287-2220
WIEST Avis 820 5th St W 284-3750
WIEST Dale (Thelma) (B) 287-2292
WIEST Don (Evelyn) 610 Student Dr 284-4136
WIEST Fred J (Lurea) (Box 164) (B) 287-2415
WILDER Harold (G) 352-4084
WILKENING Walter 612 Highland Dr 284-3989
WILKINSON Terry (Kathy) 620 H Street W 284-2160
WILKINSON Tom (Omega) 1445 11th St E 284-6307
WILLEY Charles (Bonnie) RR 1 284-4909
WILLEY Danny (Lillie) 711 8th St W 284-6853
WILLEY David (Helen) (Box 147) (K) 726-2256
WILLEY Elmer (Ella) 118 D Street W 284-2684
WILLIAMS Albert (Ozeal E) RR 2 284-2630
WILLIAMS Bill RR 2 284-6564
WILLIAMS D E (Katherine) 715 4th St E 284-2994
WILLIAMS D E Sr (LM) 284-4536
WILLIAMS Edwin P (Katherine M)
351 Valley View Dr 284-3810

WILLIAMS Martin RR 2 284-2273
WILLIAMS Walter (K) 726-2863
WILSON Arthur (Mabel A) 1801 1st St E 284-3344
WILSON Dan (Iva) 714 6th St W 284-3238
WILSON David D 901 3rd St E 284-2639
WILSON Emory E (Ruby) 1211 Candace Dr 284-3069
WILSON Everett (Lew) 355-3152
WILSON Gale 'Butch' (Dixie) RR 1 284-2501
WILSON Helen 217 A Street W 284-2484
WILSON Kenneth D (Louise) 1220 3rd St E 284-2344
WILSON Leonard 'Boe' (Doris) RR 1 284-4510
WILSON Marie RR 1 284-6988
WILSON Nancy Triple C Trlr Ct (G) 352-4604
WILSON Randy (B Sp) 889-3330
WILSON Rex (G) 352-4506
WILSON Richard B RR 2 (R) 284-6854
WILSON Richard N (Nadine) 413 5th St E 284-3204
WILSON Verne (G) 352-4364
WILSON W F 423 6th St W (G) 352-4530
WILSON Winifred M Hillcrest Trlr Pk 284-4703
WINFREE Charlie RR 2 284-2305
WINTERQUIST Clifford 840 Sherman Av (G) 352-4288
WIRTH Gunter A (Barbara) 1004 6th St E 284-4693
WISE George (Marcia) 618 4th St W 284-4806
WISEMAN Berget (Tressie) 802 G Street W 284-4618
WITKOWSKI Emma 715 H Street W 284-4870
WITKOWSKI Paul 715 H Street W 284-4870
WITKOWSKI Ronald D (Sue) 1014 H Street E 284-3019
WITT J L (June) 615 4th St E 284-3142
WITTENBERGER L J (Mabel) 820 Spruce N 284-4617
WITTIG Arnold (L) 355-3001
WLASCHIN Leonard (Tena) Lakeside Trlr Ct 284-4963
WLASCHIN Pete 710 4th St W 284-2927
WLODARCZYK Michael Mrs 704 4th St E 284-3342
WOITALEWICZ Steve 404 9th St E (G) 352-4384
WOLFE A E (Irene) 909 Central 284-3104
WOLFE Ronald D (Sandra) 1140 Highland Dr 284-2809
WOLLEN John Mrs (Box 84) (B) 287-2115
WOLVIN Phillip 'Ron' (Lucille) 1106 Robin Ln .. 284-3902
WOOD Bruce K (Naomi) (B Sp) 889-3295
WOOD Clarence (Jennie) RR 2 (B Sp) 889-3519
WOOD Danny (Merrita) RR 2 284-2659
WOOD Don 117 5th St W (G) 352-2193
WOOD Evelyn J 913 St Mary's Av 284-3292
WOOD Evelyn J 'Children's Phone 913 St Mary's Av .. 284-6205
WOOD Everett (Leota) 922 Highland Dr 284-3993
WOOD George (L) 355-2402
WOOD Grace E (G) 352-4065
WOOD Grace E 720 Lincoln Av (G) 352-4827
WOOD John L (Mary Beth) 603 8th St W 284-3220
WOOD Merrita (L) 355-3241
WOOD Stanton R (B Sp) 889-3220
WOODEN Dick 511 West Lawn Dr 284-6815
WOODHEAD Wallace 605 Sherman Av (G) 352-4743
WOODMAN J H (L) 355-2401
WOODMANCY Vern (G) 352-4297
WOODRUM S M 703 2nd St E 284-6514
WOODS Edward 510 H Street W 284-6893
WOODS James T 710 Spruce N (Apt. 1) 284-3264

WRAGE Jerry (Margaret) (K) 726-2721
WRAY Nial 312 C Street W 284-4165
WRIGHT Raymond E 844 Logan (G) 352-4317
WUJEK Stanley (Laverna) 210 5th St W 284-2600
WURST Wilbur W 402 6th St W 284-4252
WURTH Harvey H (Rose) 916 G Street W 284-2456
WYATT Mike (G) 352-4127
WYETT Caroline 418 F Street E (Apt. 6) 284-4751
WYKERT Dwayne 839 Garfield Av (G) 352-4446
WYKERT Kendall (G) 352-4417

Y

YAW E E DR phys & surg (ofc)
115 3rd St W (G)Grant Clinic 352-4424
YEATMAN Sandy 701 7th St W 284-6975
YERGER George 707 Logan (G) 889-3224
YETTER CO RR 1 (B Sp) 889-3552
YETTER Herbert C (Winifred) (Box 172) (B Sp) .. 287-2188
YETTER Sam RR 1 (B) 284-4266
YOCHUM David G Rev 602 Student Dr 355-2432
YOUNG David (L) 355-3262
YOUNG Greg (Rita) 817 10th St W 284-6277
YOUNG Nurdin (Os) 355-3262
YOUNG Philip H (Anna) 319 C Street W 284-2262
YOUNG R M (Maxine) RR 2 (R) 284-3506
YOUNG Rodney L RR 2 284-6984
YOUNG Wayne (Lorraine) 611 10th St E 284-3734
YOUNG Wendell 619 4th St W (G) 352-4925
YOUNKER Andrew (Mable) RR 2 284-3582

Z

ZABEL Herman (Megan) RR 2 (B Sp) 889-3448
ZABEL John (Ina) (B Sp) 889-3256
ZADINA Leslie RR 2 284-4889
ZAMUDIO Thomas (Susan) 614 6th St W 284-2848
ZEHR Margot 911 West Lawn Dr 284-4692
ZEHR Roger (Margot) 911 West Lawn Dr 284-4692
ZIEGLER Albert (Mary) 1801 1st St E 284-2389
ZIEGLER Clarence (Marie) 1003 4th St E 284-4184
ZIEGLER Ronald (K) 726-2801
ZIERLIEN Lulu (Lew) 355-3272
ZIGLER Ora 207 M Street E 284-3827
ZIMMERMAN Dennis (Judy) RR 2 (B Sp) 889-3431
ZIMMERMAN Elvin 1115 H Street E 284-3013
ZIMMERMAN George (Lois) RR 2 (B Sp) 889-3410
ZIMMERMAN Julia RR 2 (B Sp) 889-3180
ZIMMERMAN Ralph (Opal) RR 2 (B Sp) 889-3377
ZINGG John (G) 352-4492
ZINGG Robert (Noreen) (B) 287-2275
ZION LUTHERAN CHURCH (B Sp) 889-3632
ZION LUTHERAN CHURCH-PASTOR'S RESIDENCE
(B Sp) 889-3234
ZION LUTHERAN-PARSONAGE 115 7th St E (G) .. 352-4565

1. Estimate:

a. the number of phones in this city; _____

b. the population of the city (you'll need more information); _____

c. the number of businesses in the city. _____

2. Discuss:

a. why your estimates may be inaccurate;

b. ways of making them more accurate.

• *Sampling a large population*
• *Developing problem-solving strategies*
• *Working with ratios*

Name _____

Advanced Calculator Math

Copyright © 1980 by Fearon Pitman Publishers, Inc.

3-43

Friends

Working with patterns in numbers

1. Three people give each other Christmas presents. How many presents all together? What if there had been 4 people? Fill in the chart.

For experts:

Can you find a formula that gives the number of presents for any group of people?

Number of People	Number of Presents
2	2
3	
4	
5	
6	
8	
10	
18	

2. Three people are introduced to each other and shake hands. How many handshakes all together? What if there had been 4 people? Make a chart to show the number of handshakes for other groups.

For experts:

Can you find a formula that gives the number of handshakes for any group of people?

Number of People	Number of Shakes
2	1
3	
4	
5	
6	
8	
10	
18	

• *Developing algebraic reasoning*

Name _____

3-44

Remainders and the Calculator: Part I

What that decimal remainder means

1. Work out longhand. Leave a remainder. The first one is done for you.

a. $4\overline{)30}$ with quotient 7 R2, 28, remainder 2

b. $5\overline{)23}$

c. $8\overline{)46}$

d. $4\overline{)38}$

2. Work out longhand. Use decimals. Check with your calculator. The first one is done for you.

a. $4\overline{)30.0}$ with quotient 7.5, 28, 20, 20, 0

b. $5\overline{)23.0}$

c. $8\overline{)46.00}$

d. $4\overline{)38.0}$

Compare **1a** and **2a**.
Think of a way to use the decimal quotient for finding the remainder.

$$\begin{array}{r} 7.5 \\ \times\ 4 \\ \hline 30.0 \end{array}$$

or

$$7.5 \times 4 = (7 + 0.5) \times 4 = (7 \times 4) + (0.5 \times 4)$$
$$= 28 + 2 \quad \text{Remainder}$$
$$= 30$$

Think of a way to use your calculator for finding the remainder from the decimal quotient. Write down which buttons you push to check the remainder for (b), (c), and (d).

_____

_____

_____

_____

• *Developing calculator algorithms*
• *Developing mathematical reasoning*
• *Reviewing inverse operations*

Name _____

Advanced Calculator Math

Copyright © 1980 by Fearon Pitman Publishers, Inc.

3-45

Remainders and the Calculator: Part II

Decimals to remainders an easy way

1. Find the whole number remainder for the following:

$$\begin{array}{r} 6.5 \\ 6\overline{)39} \end{array} \qquad \begin{array}{r} 10.75 \\ 4\overline{)43} \end{array} \qquad \begin{array}{r} 12.4 \\ 5\overline{)62} \end{array}$$

R =   R =   R =

$384 \div 15 = 25.6$. What whole number remainder does the 0.6 stand for? _____

2. Find a method for determining the whole number remainder without clearing the calculator.

Try: $434 \div 35$ **Answer:**   _____
Whole number part :   _____
Fractional part :   _____
Whole number remainder :   _____

Your steps should be:

       (   )
Display

3. Write the quotient and remainder for the following.
The first one is done for you. Use your calculator.

	Quotient	**Remainder**
17 ÷ 2	8.5	1
23 ÷ 4		
184 ÷ 16		
200 ÷ 10		
163 ÷ 8		
4403 ÷ 136		
1239 ÷ 42		
6734 ÷ 185		

• *Developing calculator algorithms*
• *Developing mathematical reasoning*
• *Reviewing inverse operations*

3-46

Remainders and the Calculator: Part III

Testing your skills with remainders

1. Multiply. Work out longhand.

$$\frac{1}{3} \times 3 \qquad\qquad \frac{4}{9} \times 9 \qquad\qquad \frac{2}{3} \times 6$$

= _____   = _____   = _____

2. Change to decimals.

$$\frac{1}{3} = \text{_____} \qquad \frac{4}{9} = \text{_____} \qquad \frac{2}{3} = \text{_____}$$

3. Repeat the questions of problem 1, using your calculator.

$$\frac{1}{3} \times 3 \qquad\qquad \frac{4}{9} \times 9 \qquad\qquad \frac{2}{3} \times 6$$

= _____   = _____   = _____

4. Compare the answers to questions 1 and 3. Which are right?

_____

| When the calculator shows 0.9999999, it usually means 1. |

5. Find the quotient and whole number remainder for the following division problems.

	Quotient	Remainder
62 ÷ 3	_____	_____
73 ÷ 9	_____	_____
84 ÷ 13	_____	_____
127 ÷ 7	_____	_____
135 ÷ 19	_____	_____
236 ÷ 21	_____	_____
6087 ÷ 89	_____	_____
2111 ÷ 17	_____	_____

• *Developing calculator algorithms*
• *Developing mathematical reasoning*
• *Reviewing inverse operations*

Name _____

Answer Key

This section provides solutions for all sheets having exact answers. In estimation exercises, the students' approximations are more important than the exact answers, and the exact answers given here should be de-emphasized. Some sheets have no answers; these are noted in sequence in this section for easy reference.

3-1

The Cost of Money: Part I

Simple interest—how much you pay

Work through the following example.

Example 1   Solution

Deposit or Loan (Principal) :	$100	8% of $100 = 0.08 × $100 = $8
Interest Rate :	8%	Interest = $8
Interest after 1 year =	*$8*	Total owing = $100 (principal) + $8 (interest)
Total owing after 1 year =	*$108*	= $108

The calculator is able to do this type of question. Look at Example 1 again. Punch in:

[1] [0] [0] [+] [8] [%]   The display shows "8." This is the interest. Push [=]

The display shows "108." This is the total (principal + interest). Try Example 1 again.

It is possible to find the total (principal + interest) in one step, without using the % key.
For Example 1, the steps would be: [1] [0] [0] [×] [1] [.] [0] [8] [=]

100% (principal) + 8% (interest)

The display would read "108," the total.
By subtracting the principal (100), you can find the interest (108 − 100 = 8).

1.
Principal :	$250
Interest Rate :	9%
Interest :	*$22.50*
Total Owing (after 1 year) :	*$272.50*

2. Find the value after 1 year of :
$87.49 invested at 9% : *$95.36*
$2645 invested at 12% : *$2962.40*

3.
Principal	Rate	Interest	Total After 1 year
$ 460.00	4%	*$18.40*	*$478.40*
$ 625.49	9%	*$56.29*	*$681.78*
$4000.00	11%	*$440.00*	*$4440.00*
$ 256.33	7%	*$17.94*	*$274.27*
$5847.00	9.5%	*$555.47*	*$6402.47*

Name _____

• *Introducing the % key*
• *Using the calculator effectively*
• *Building consumer awareness*

3-2

The Cost of Money: Part II

More on calculating simple interest

Money is often borrowed or deposited for longer periods of time. In these cases,
simple interest is computed on the original amount (the principal) every year.

Example   Solution

Principal :	$300	Interest for 1 year = $300 × 0.06
Interest Rate :	6%	= $18
Loan Period :	4 years	Interest for 4 years = $18 × 4
Interest per year =	*$18.00*	= $72
Interest for 4 years :	*$72.00*	Total = $300 + $72
Interest + principal :	*$372.00*	= $372

Fast Method

Push [3] [0] [0] [+] [6] [%]   [=] [=] [=] [=]

4 years

$867.99

1. Interest Rate : 14%
   Period : 2 years
   Total Payable : *$1111.03*

2. Interest Rate : 7%
   Period : 4 years
   Total after 4 years : *$3160.32*

$2469.00 (savings account)

3.
Principal	Rate	Period	Interest	Total Payable
$ 420.25	12 %	3 years	*$151.29*	*$571.54*
$1200.72	9.5%	5 years	*$570.34*	*$1771.06*
$1935.72	14 %	15 years	*$4065.01*	*$6000.73*
$ 318.75	10 %	12 years	*$382.50*	*$701.25*
$ 100.00	18 %	50 years	*$900.00*	*$1000.00*

Name _____

• *Introducing the % key*
• *Using the calculator effectively*
• *Building consumer awareness*

3-3

The State's Little Bit Extra

Figuring sales tax

1. a. Assuming a sales tax of 7%, find the total cost for articles priced as follows:

Cost	Cost + Sales Tax
$ 7.00	$7.49
$12.00	12.84
$ 8.00	8.56
$ 2.00	2.14
$ 4.70	5.03
Total Bill	**$36.06**

b. Now find the total cost without any sales tax first. Then calculate the tax for that total amount. $36.06 (no difference)

c. Is the total bill any different?

d. This is an illustration of the distributive property.
Explain. $1.07 \times \$33.70 = (1.07 \times \$7) + (1.07 \times \$12) + (1.07 \times \$8) + (1.07 \times \$2) + (1.07 \times \$4.70)$

2. a. Assuming a sales tax of 6%, find the total bill for a set of articles priced as follows:

Cost	Cost + Sales Tax
$ 5.00	$5.30
$ 4.80	5.09
$ 2.44	2.59
$ 7.30	7.74
$ 5.60	5.94
Total Bill	**$26.66**

b. Now use the calculator to find the total cost first and then add the sales tax.

c. Is there a difference? Explain. $26.65 (yes, a difference of $.01)

d. Which method of calculating the total bill is fairer? Why?
The second method ($26.65). In the first method, it is possible that the accumulated errors from rounding will eventually total enough to cause a difference in cost (in this case $.01).

_____

_____

* Using the % key
* Understanding taxation

13

3-4

Money, Money in the Bank: Part I

Understanding compound interest

1. Joan's grandfather gave her $100.00 to open a savings account.
At the end of each year, the bank pays 6% interest and adds it to the account.
Fill in the table to show how Joan's account increases.

Principal: $100   Interest Rate: 6%   Term: 5 years (compound interest)

	Principal $		Interest $		Total $
Year 1	100	+	$100 \times 0.06 = 6$	=	$100 + 6 = 106$
Year 2	106	+	6.36	=	112.36
Year 3	112.36	+	6.74	=	119.10
Year 4	119.10	+	7.15	=	126.25
Year 5	126.25	+	7.58	=	133.83

Interest which is added to the account each year to form the principal for the following year is called *compound interest.*

What is the difference between simple interest and compound interest?
You pay interest on last year's interest on interest

Which is more? *compound* Why? *interest on interest*

Which is fairer? *compound ???*

2. Fill in the table.

Principal: $100   Rate: 7%   Term: 6 years

	Principal $	Principal + Interest (Total) $
Year 1	100	107
Year 2	107	114.49
Year 3	114.49	122.50
Year 4	122.50	131.08
Year 5	131.08	140.25
Year 6	140.25	150.07

* Using the % key
* Understanding compound interest
* Using the calculator effectively

14

3-5

Money, Money in the Bank: Part II

How compound interest adds up

1. Fill in the table.

Principal: $100   Rate of Interest: 8%   Loan Period: 5 years

Principal + Interest Method A

(1 0 0 + 8 % =)
= = = =

Principal + Interest Method B

1 0 0 × 1 . 0 8 =
= = = =

Years	Method A	Method B
1	108.00	108.00
2	116.00	116.64
3	124.00	125.97
4	132.00	136.05
5	140.00	146.93

2. Discuss the differences between the two methods and answers.

A. *simple interest*

B. *compound interest*

3. Use the methods shown above to fill in this table.

Principal	Rate	Period	Total (Simple Interest)	Total (Compound Interest)
$400	7%	2 years	456.00	457.96
$960	12%	3 years	1305.60	1348.73
$1435	15%	5 years	2511.25	2886.30
$2869	18%	7 years	6483.94	9139.12
$5000	10%	10 years	10,000.00	12,968.71

4. The family Mark babysat for was so pleased with his work that they promised and paid him a 10% increase over the previous year's rate at each of his birthdays. Mark decided to make a career out of babysitting for this family. He sat for nieces and nephews, then for the children's children, and finally for great-grandchildren. He started at age 12 for $1.00 per hour. At age 85, he was still sitting for the same family. What was his hourly rate at that time? *$1051.15*

• *Using the % key*
• *Understanding compound interest*

Name _____

3-6

How Fast Can You Estimate?

Rounding helps you figure faster

Estimate by rounding each number to a multiple of 5 or 10 before adding or subtracting.

1.

18 + 5 + 13 − 23 + 2 + 7 − 11 =	11
75 − 27 + 57 − 78 − 42 + 14 − 2 =	−3
24 − 37 + 2 + 19 − 13 + 86 + 61 =	142
78 + 89 − 5 − 68 + 1 + 14 − 53 =	56
82 − 68 + 7 + 6 − 8 + 24 + 4 =	47

2.

267 + 691 − 52 − 152 + 311 − 8 − 86 =	971
49 + 306 + 89 − 81 − 59 + 631 − 90 =	847
82 − 72 + 129 + 516 − 78 − 558 + 29 =	48
951 − 926 + 82 + 54 − 16 − 27 − 19 =	99
56 + 76 + 59 − 65 − 3 − 22 + 98 =	199

3.

389 + 93 − 652 + 218 − 62 =	−14
96 + 21 − 126 − 235 + 540 =	296
12 − 71 + 825 − 54 − 77 =	635
232 − 26 + 323 − 983 + 230 =	−224
324 − 790 + 3 + 913 − 894 =	−444

Estimates will vary.

Check your estimates with a calculator.

Put a check mark beside any estimate that is within 50 of the exact answer.

Put a star beside any estimate that is within 10 of the exact answer.

• *Reviewing estimation and rounding*
• *Rounding to the nearest five or ten*
• *Estimating positive and negative integers*

Name _____

3-8
All-Star Estimating
Think about the decimals first

Estimate each product to at least 2 significant digits.

Exact answers given. Estimates may vary.

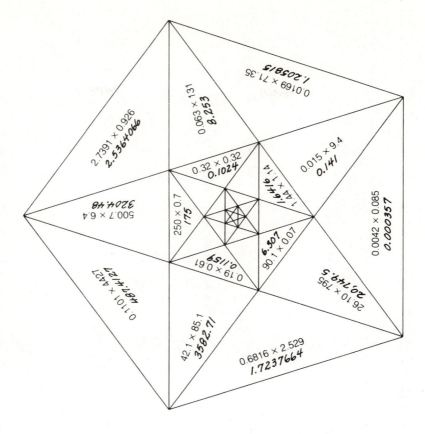

Sheet 3-7

Check your estimates with your calculator.

• *Rounding with decimals*
• *Estimating in multiplication*

18

Name _____

Triangles A, D, E, G, H, and I are the "Bermuda" Triangles.

3-9
Divide and Figure
Will rounding help you?

Circle the answer which is the best estimate for each quotient.
The first one is done for you.

1.
a.	2822 ÷ 24	(100)	150	200
b.	1632 ÷ 47	(40)	70	100
c.	7965 ÷ 94	60	(80)	100
d.	1338 ÷ 82	10	(15)	20
e.	2248 ÷ 73	10	20	(30)

2.
f.	3777 ÷ 15	150	200	(250)
g.	6345 ÷ 62	50	(100)	150
h.	1066 ÷ 95	(10)	20	50
i.	2790 ÷ 98	10	(30)	50
j.	4008 ÷ 86	10	30	(50)

3.
k.	5054 ÷ 53	50	(100)	150
l.	8492 ÷ 21	200	300	(400)
m.	1426 ÷ 69	10	(20)	30
n.	2396 ÷ 84	10	20	(30)
o.	4026 ÷ 69	40	(60)	80

4.
p.	8425 ÷ 54	100	(150)	200
q.	1336 ÷ 35	(40)	60	80
r.	1909 ÷ 90	10	15	(20)
s.	7439 ÷ 32	(200)	300	400
t.	5388 ÷ 93	(50)	75	100

Check your estimates with the calculator.

Sheet 3-10 through Sheet 3-15
No specific answers.

• *Reviewing estimation in division*
• *Rounding in division*

Name _____

_____ 19

3-16
A Decimal by Another Name
Converting decimals to fractions

If you were to divide 312 by 4 and multiply your answer by 4 again, what do you think your answer would be? **312**
Try it on your calculator.

If you were to divide any counting number by 4 and multiply your answer by 4 again, what do you think your answer would be? **The same number**
Try it on your calculator. Write down 5 examples. **Answers will vary.**

a. $6÷4×4=6$ **b.** $95÷4×4=95$ **c.** $82÷4×4=82$ **d.** *etc.* **e.** ___

A number is divided by 4. The answer is 1.25. What was the original number? **5**

A number is divided by 8. The result is 0.375. What was the original number? **3**

0.375 equals what fraction? $\frac{3}{8}$ *(i.e., 3÷8)*

A number is divided by 25. The result is 0.92. What was the number that was divided by 25? **23**

The decimal fraction $0.92 = \frac{23}{25}$.

Change the following decimal fractions to fractions with the required denominator.

$0.3 = \frac{3}{10}$ $0.4 = \frac{2}{5}$ $0.75 = \frac{3}{4}$ $0.3125 = \frac{5}{16}$ $0.625 = \frac{5}{8}$

$0.095 = \frac{19}{200}$ $0.6 = \frac{9}{15}$ $0.064 = \frac{8}{125}$ $0.2125 = \frac{17}{80}$ $0.75 = \frac{24}{32}$

From the problems, you can show that $\frac{3}{4} = \frac{24}{32}$. How?

$\frac{3}{4} = 0.75, \frac{24}{32} = 0.75, \text{therefore}, \frac{3}{4} = \frac{24}{32}$

Without using the table, you might still change $\frac{3}{4}$ to $\frac{24}{32}$ by thinking

$\frac{3}{4} = 0.75 = \frac{?}{32}$

• *Converting decimals to fractions*
• *Working with equivalent fractions*

Name ___

26

3-17
It's All Equal
No-sweat fraction alterations

Use your calculator to change $\frac{3}{5}$ to another fraction with denominator 25.

The answer should be $\frac{3}{5} = \frac{15}{25}$

Similarly, change the following fractions to equivalent forms.

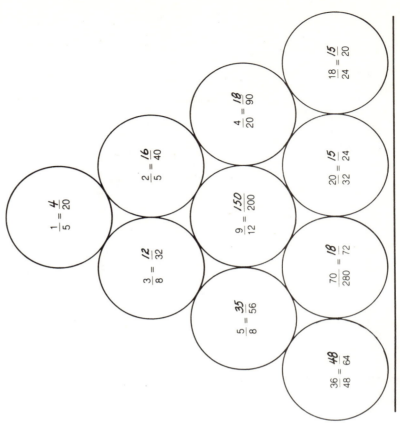

$\frac{1}{5} = \frac{4}{20}$

$\frac{3}{8} = \frac{12}{32}$

$\frac{2}{5} = \frac{16}{40}$

$\frac{5}{8} = \frac{35}{56}$

$\frac{9}{12} = \frac{150}{200}$

$\frac{4}{20} = \frac{18}{90}$

$\frac{36}{48} = \frac{48}{64}$

$\frac{70}{280} = \frac{18}{72}$

$\frac{20}{32} = \frac{15}{24}$

$\frac{18}{24} = \frac{15}{20}$

• *Converting fractions to decimals*
• *Working with equivalent fractions*

Name ___

27

3-18
The Calculating Fraction: Part I
How a calculator handles fractions

Most calculators are not capable of showing common fractions on their displays. Therefore, common fractions are usually changed to decimals for calculators.

Exercise A

Change to decimal fractions. (You may use your calculator if don't remember these yet.)

$\frac{1}{2}$ = __0.5__ $\frac{5}{8}$ = __0.625__

$\frac{3}{4}$ = __0.75__

How would you compute the decimal fraction for $\frac{27}{45}$? __27 ÷ 45__

Exercise B

Add, showing all work.
Change your answer to a decimal fraction.

$\frac{2}{5} + \frac{3}{4}$ = _____

Your work should look something like this:

$\frac{2}{5} + \frac{3}{4} = \frac{2 \times 4}{5 \times 4} + \frac{3 \times 5}{4 \times 5}$

$= \frac{8}{20} + \frac{15}{20}$

$= \frac{23}{20}$

$= 1\frac{3}{20}$

$= 1\frac{15}{100}$

$= 1.15$

It would be easy to change each fraction to a decimal first, and then add. For example:

$\frac{2}{5} + \frac{3}{4} = 0.4 + 0.75$ 0.4
                 0.75

           = 1.15   1.15

Exercise C

Try these. (Write the intermediate steps, as in the example.)

1. $\frac{3}{4} + \frac{7}{8}$ = _____

2. $\frac{1}{2} + \frac{7}{16}$ = _____

Your work should look like this:

1. $\frac{3}{4} + \frac{7}{8} = 0.75 + 0.875$

     = 1.625

2. $\frac{1}{2} + \frac{7}{16} = 0.5 + 0.4375$

     = 0.9375

Note: Teach mini-lesson here. (See Teacher's Guide.)

Exercise D

Now try these. Show your work.

1. $\frac{9}{25} + \frac{36}{64} = 0.36 + 0.5625$

     = 0.9225

2. $\frac{15}{24} + \frac{35}{40} = 0.625 + 0.875$

     = 1.5

Sheet 3-19

Answers for this sheet are printed on the sheet for immediate student reference.

- Adding and subtracting common fractions
- Using the calculator optimally
- Working with the distributive property
- Working with calculator algorithms

Name _____

3-21
Be a Number Detective: Part I

Can you predict the patterns?

1. Use your calculator: Predict:

$1 \div 3 =$ 0.3333333 $1000 \div \underline{3333} = \underline{0.3000300}$

$10 \div 33 =$ 0.3030303 $10,000 \div \underline{33,333} = \underline{0.3000030}$

$100 \div 333 =$ 0.300303 $100,000 \div \underline{333,333} = \underline{0.3000003}$

Check your guesses.

2. Use your calculator: Predict:

$1 \div 7 =$ 0.1428571 $4 \div 7 = \underline{0.5714285}$

$2 \div 7 =$ 0.2857142 $5 \div 7 = \underline{0.7142857}$

$3 \div 7 =$ 0.4285714 $6 \div 7 = \underline{0.8571428}$

Hint: look at the order of the digits.

3. Use your calculator: Predict:

$1 \times 9 =$ 9

$11 \times 99 =$ 1089 $11,111 \times 99,999 = \underline{1,111,088,889}$

$111 \times 999 =$ $110,889$ $111,111 \times 999,999 = \underline{111,110,888889}$

$1111 \times 9999 =$ $11,108,889$ *(The underlined digits are beyond the calculator display.)*

• *Detecting and completing patterns*

Name _____

3-20
Fast Fractions

How you help your calculator do it

Exercise A

1. $\frac{3}{7} \times 4 =$ **2.** $\frac{2}{5} \times 12 =$

3. $5 \times \frac{2}{9} =$ **4.** $8 \times \frac{4}{3} =$

Answers: 1. 1.7142857   2. 4.8   3. 1.1111111   4. 10.666666

Find a way to do $\frac{7}{10} \times \frac{5}{8}$ on your machine. Your answer should be 0.4375.

One way is $\boxed{7}$ $\times$ $\boxed{5}$ $\div$ $\boxed{10}$ $\div$ $\boxed{8}$

Exercise B

1. $\frac{5}{6} \times \frac{9}{10} =$ **2.** $\frac{3}{4} \times \frac{5}{8} =$ **3.** $\frac{3}{8} \times \frac{7}{5} =$

4. $\frac{4}{14} \times \frac{7}{4} =$ **5.** $\frac{13}{29} \times \frac{5}{26} =$

Answers: 1. 0.75   2. 0.46875   3. 0.525   4. 0.5   5. 0.0862068

Exercise C

1. $\frac{5}{8} \times \frac{4}{6} \times \frac{9}{10} =$ **2.** $\frac{7}{16} \times \frac{2}{5} \times \frac{5}{12} =$

3. $\frac{5}{6} \times \frac{5}{8} \times \frac{33}{8} =$ **4.** $\frac{4}{15} \times \frac{5}{26} \times \frac{100}{3} =$

Answers: 1. 0.375   2. 0.0729166   3. 2.1484375   4. 1.7094016

• *Using the calculator optimally*
• *Multiplying fractions*
• *Working with calculator algorithms*

Name _____

3-22
Be a Number Detective: Part II
More patterns to figure out

$$1 = 1 = 1^2$$
$$1+3 = 4 = 2^2$$
$$1+3+5 = 9 = 3^2$$
$$1+3+5+7 = 16 = 4^2$$
$$1+3+5+7+9 = 25 = 5^2$$
$$1+3+5+7+9+11 = 36 = 6^2$$
$$1+3+5+7+9+11+13 = 49 = 7^2$$
$$\text{Guess: } 1+3+5+\ldots+19 = 100 = 10^2$$

1. To understand what is happening, count the number of dots in each section of the square.

(diagram labeled 1, 3, 5, 7, 9, 11)

However, the whole figure is a square containing 6 × 6 dots.
Therefore, $1 + 3 + 5 + 7 + 9 + 11 = 6^2$.

2. Complete the diagram below to illustrate the sum
$$1 + 3 + 5 + 7 + 9 + 11 + 13 + 15.$$

(diagram labeled 1, 3, 5, 7, 9, 11, 13, 15)

Write the corresponding number sentence.
$$1+3+5+7+9+11+13+15 = 64 = 8^2$$

Use your calculator to check whether $1 + 3 + 5 + 7 + \ldots + 31$ is a perfect square.

Yes $256 = 16^2$

Name _____

- *Detecting and completing patterns*
- *Explaining patterns*
- *Squaring and square root*

32

3-23
Be a Square Detective
Showing squares with dot patterns

$$1 = 1 = 1^2$$
$$1+2+1 = 4 = 2^2$$
$$1+2+3+2+1 = 9 = 3^2$$
$$1+2+3+4+3+2+1 = 16 = 4^2$$
$$1+2+3+4+5+4+3+2+1 = 25 = 5^2$$
$$1+2+3+4+5+6+5+4+3+2+1 = 36 = 6^2$$

Now guess:
$$1+2+3+4+5+6+7+8+9+10+9+8+7+6+5+4+3+2+1 = 100 = 10^2$$

1. Use this dot pattern to explain what is happening.

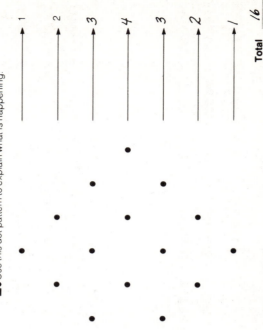

Arrows labeled: 1, 2, 3, 4, 3, 2, 1 Total 16

But the whole figure is a square containing 4 × 4 = (4)² dots.
Therefore, $1 + 2 + 3 + 4 + 3 + 2 + 1 = 16$.

2. Draw a similar dot diagram to explain why
$$1 + 2 + 3 + 4 + 5 + 4 + 3 + 2 + 1 = 5^2.$$

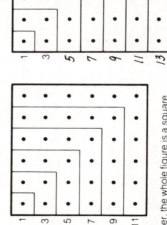

Name _____

- *Detecting and explaining patterns*
- *Squaring and square root*

33

3-24
The Three-Angle Detective

Dot patterns for triangles

1	=	1
1 + 2	=	3
1 + 2 + 3	=	6
1 + 2 + 3 + 4	=	10
1 + 2 + 3 + 4 + 5	=	15
1 + 2 + 3 + 4 + 5 + 6	=	21
1 + 2 + 3 + 4 + 5 + 6 + 7	=	28

The numbers 1, 3, 6, 10, etc., are called triangular numbers.
Look at the dot pattern to see why.

What seems to happen when one triangular number is added to the next one?
A square is formed.

Explain, using the dot pattern below.

The two triangular arrays combine to form a square array. The bottom row
of the larger triangular array forms a diagonal of the square.

· Detecting and completing patterns
· Explaining patterns
· Squaring and square root

Name _____

34

3-25
Pattern Power

Can you explain these patterns?

1.
6 × 9	=	54
6 × 99	=	594
6 × 999	=	5994
6 × 9999	=	59,994
6 × 99,999	=	599,994
6 × 999,999	=	5,999,994

2.
9 × 6	=	54
9 × 66	=	594
9 × 666	=	5994
9 × 6666	=	59,994
9 × 66,666	=	599,994
9 × 666,666	=	5,999,994

Compare your answers for 1 and 2. Explain:
The number on the left side of the multiplication sign is multiplied by $\frac{3}{2}$;
the number on the right side of the multiplication sign is divided by $\frac{3}{2}$.
Or: $6 \times 9999 = (2 \times 3) \times (3 \times 3333) = (3 \times 3) \times (2 \times 3333) = 9 \times 6666$

3.
4 × 2	=	8
4 × 22	=	88
4 × 222	=	888
4 × 2222	=	8888
4 × 22,222	=	88,888
4 × 222,222	=	888,888

4.
2 × 4	=	8
2 × 44	=	88
2 × 444	=	888
2 × 4444	=	8888
2 × 44,444	=	88,888
2 × 444,444	=	888,888

Compare your answers for 3 and 4. Explain:
The number on the left side of the multiplication sign is divided by 2;
the number on the right side of the multiplication sign is multiplied by 2.
Or: $4 \times 2222 = (2 \times 2) \times 2222 = 2 \times (2 \times 2222) = 2 \times 4444$.

5. Pick any two 1-digit numbers (say, 3 and 8). Form a pattern like those on this page.

3 × 8	=	8 × 3 =
3 × 88	=	8 × 33 =
⋮		⋮

Compare the answers. Explain. Try another example.

· Detecting patterns
· Explaining patterns
· Understanding number properties
· Developing algebraic reasoning

Name _____

35

3-27
Super Pattern Power

See if you can explain these

1.
$1 \times 7 \times 11 \times 13 = \underline{1001}$
$2 \times 7 \times 11 \times 13 = \underline{2002}$
$3 \times 7 \times 11 \times 13 = \underline{3003}$
$4 \times 7 \times 11 \times 13 = \underline{4004}$

Explain: $\underline{7 \times 11 \times 13 = 1001}$

$\underline{6 \times (7 \times 11 \times 13) = 6 \times 1001 = 6006}$

2.
$1 \div 11 = \underline{0.090909}$
$2 \div 11 = \underline{0.181818}$
$3 \div 11 = \underline{0.272727}$
$4 \div 11 = \underline{0.363636}$
$\underline{5} \div 11 = \underline{0.454545}$
$6 \div 11 = \underline{0.545454}$

Explain: $\underline{1 \div 11 = 0.090909}$

$\underline{6 \div 11 = 6 \times (1 \div 11) = 6 \times 0.090909}$
$\underline{ = 0.545454}$

3.
$12,345,679 \times \quad 9 = \underline{111,111,111}$
$12,345,679 \times \ 18 = \underline{222,222,222}$
$12,345,679 \times \ 27 = \underline{333,333,333}$
$12,345,679 \times \ 36 = \underline{444,444,444}$
$12,345,679 \times \ 45 = \underline{555,555,555}$
$12,345,679 \times \ 54 = \underline{666,666,666}$

Explain: $\underline{12,345,679 \times 9 = 111,111,111}$

$\underline{12,345,679 \times 63 = 12,345,679 \times (9 \times 7)}$
$\underline{= (12,345,679 \times 9) \times 7 = 111,111,111 \times 7 = 777,777,777}$

4.
$2 + 4 \qquad\qquad = \quad 6 = 2 \times 3$
$2 + 4 + 6 \qquad\ = \ 12 = 3 \times 4$
$2 + 4 + 6 + 8 \quad = \ \underline{20} = \underline{4 \times 5}$
$2 + 4 + 6 + 8 + 10 = \underline{30} = \underline{5 \times 6}$

Use the array of blocks to explain why
$2 + 4 + 6 + 8 + 10 = 5 \times 6$.

$\underline{A\ cut\text{-}out\ of\ the\ shaded}$
$\underline{part\ fits\ beside\ the}$
$\underline{lower\ piece\ to\ form\ a}$
$\underline{5 \times 6\ rectangle.}$

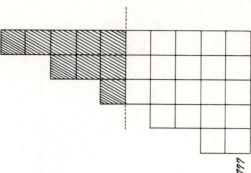

• *Detecting patterns*
• *Explaining patterns*
• *Understanding number properties*
• *Developing algebraic reasoning*

Name _____

3-26
More Pattern Power

More exploration of patterns

1. Store any 1-digit number in your calculator.
Multiply by 3. Multiply by 37.
Compare your answer with the original number. Explain:

e.g., 5
$\quad\ \ 15$
$\quad .555$

$\underline{3 \times 37 = 111}$

$\underline{So,\ 5 \times (3 \times 37) = 5 \times 111 = 555}$

2. Store any 1-digit number in your calculator.
Multiply by 13. Multiply by 7. Multiply by 11. Multiply by 3.
Compare your answer with the starting number. Explain:

e.g., 5
$\quad\ \ 65$
$\quad 455$
$\quad 5005$
$\quad 185,185$
$\quad 555,555$

$\underline{13 \times 7 \times 11 \times 37 \times 3 = 111,111}$

$\underline{So,\ 5 \times (13 \times 7 \times 11 \times 37 \times 3) = 5 \times 111,111 = 555,555}$

3. Store any 3-digit number in your calculator.
Multiply by 13. Multiply by 7. Multiply by 11.
Compare your answer with your starting number. Explain:

e.g., 123
$\quad 1599$
$\quad 11,193$
$\quad 123,123$

$\underline{13 \times 7 \times 11 = 1001}$

$\underline{So,\ 123 \times (13 \times 7 \times 11) = 123 \times 1001 = 123,123}$

4. Store any 1-digit number in your calculator.
Multiply by 16. Multiply by 43. Multiply by 1483.
Look for the pattern in your answer. Explain:

e.g., 5
$\quad\ \ 80$
$\quad 3440$
$\quad 5,101,520$
$\quad 5,10,15,20$

$\underline{16 \times 43 \times 1483 = 1,020,304}$

$\underline{So,\ 5 \times (16 \times 43 \times 1483) = 5 \times 1,020,304 = 5,101,520}$

• *Detecting patterns*
• *Explaining patterns*
• *Understanding number properties*
• *Developing algebraic reasoning*

Name _____

36 •

68 *Advanced CALCULATOR MATH*

3-28
Just a Little Bit Closer
What is a convergent sequence?

1. Use your calculator to find the decimal equivalents of the following:

a. $\frac{1}{2} = 0.5$

b. $\frac{2}{3} = 0.\bar{6}$

c. $\frac{3}{4} = 0.75$

d. $\frac{4}{5} = 0.8$

e. $\frac{5}{6} = 0.8\bar{3}$

f. $\frac{6}{7} = 0.\overline{857142}$

g. $\frac{7}{8} = 0.875$

Write the next 3 numbers and their decimal equivalents.

h. $\frac{8}{9} = 0.\bar{8}$

i. $\frac{9}{10} = 0.9$

j. $\frac{10}{11} = 0.\overline{90}$

2. Mark the values on the number line.

0 — $\frac{1}{2}$ $\frac{2}{3}$ $\frac{3}{4}$ $\frac{4}{5}$ $\frac{5}{6}$ $\frac{7}{8}$ $\frac{6}{7}$ $\frac{8}{9}$ $\frac{9}{10}$ $\frac{10}{11}$ — 1

3. What do you notice when each term is compared to the next one?

Each number is further to the right and closer to 1.

4. To what number are the terms of the sequence getting closer and closer? 1
How can you test that guess?

By testing some additional numbers such as $\frac{86}{87}$, $\frac{233}{234}$, etc.

3-29
How Close Can You Get?
More about convergent sequences

Here is another sequence: $\frac{2}{1}, \frac{3}{2}, \frac{4}{3}, \frac{5}{4}, \ldots$

1. Again, use your calculator to find the decimal equivalents of these terms:

a. $\frac{2}{1} = 2$

b. $\frac{3}{2} = 1.5$

c. $\frac{4}{3} = 1.\bar{3}$

d. $\frac{5}{4} = 1.25$

e. $\frac{6}{5} = 1.2$

f. $\frac{7}{6} = 1.1\bar{6}$

g. $\frac{8}{7} = 1.\overline{142857}$

Find the next 3 terms in the sequence and the decimal equivalents.

h. $\frac{9}{8} = 1.125$

i. $\frac{10}{9} = 1.\bar{1}$

j. $\frac{11}{10} = 1.1$

2. Mark each term on the number line.

1 — $\frac{11}{10}$ $\frac{9}{8}$ $\frac{7}{6}$ $\frac{6}{5}$ $\frac{5}{4}$ $\frac{4}{3}$ $\frac{3}{2}$ — 2

3. What do you notice when each term in the sequence is compared to the next one?

Each number is further to the left and closer to 1.

4. What number is the sequence getting closer and closer to? 1
That number is called the limit of that sequence.

5. Can you think of a sequence which has a limit of 0? Check your guess with the calculator. What is the sequence?

$\frac{1}{2}, \frac{1}{3}, \frac{1}{4}, \frac{1}{5}, \frac{1}{6}, \ldots$ (Other answers are possible.)

6. Can you find a sequence which has a limit of $\frac{1}{2}$? Hint: The denominator may have to be at least twice as large as the numerator. (There are other ways, also.) Check with your calculator. What is the sequence?

$\frac{1}{3}, \frac{2}{5}, \frac{3}{7}, \frac{4}{9}, \frac{5}{11}, \ldots$ (There are many other possibilities.)

3-30

Paper Folding Challenge

Creases, pieces, lines, and numbers

1. A point divides a line into two parts.

Two points divide a line into how many parts?

Fill in the table to show points and parts.

Number of Points	Number of Parts
1	2
2	3
3	4
4	5
6	7
82	83

2. Fold a sheet of paper in half. Fold the paper again in the same direction as before (see the illustration). Into how many parts is the paper divided? Complete the table.

Number of Times Folded	Number of Parts	Number of Creases
1	2	1
2	4	3
3	8	7
4	16	15
5	32	31
10	1024	1023
20	1,048,576	1,048,575

3. Fold a sheet of paper in half. Fold again in the other direction. Into how many parts is the paper divided? How many crease lines go all the way across the page?

Number of Times Folded	Number of Parts	Number of Crease Lines
1	2	1
2	4	2
3	8	3
4	16	4
5	32	5
6	64	6
20	1,048,576	20

• Detecting patterns
• Developing mathematical reasoning

Name _____

40

Sheet 3-31

Answers vary depending on the data used.

3-32

Best Buys

Who's the smartest shopper?

Circle the "best buys" for each item.

Item	Brand A Size	Brand A Cost	Brand B Size	Brand B Cost
Chips	(50 g)	20¢	40 g	19¢
Onions	1 kg	39¢	(1.5 kg)	50¢
Pickles	750 mL	2 for $1.49	(800 mL)	3 for $2.09
Hamburger	800 g	$1.47	(900 g)	$1.60
Cheese	0.5 kg pack	2 packs for $1.49	(0.75 kg pack)	$1.07
Apples	(10)	98¢ a doz.	10	2 for 19¢
Jelly	50 mL	3 for 89¢	(25 mL)	7 for $1
Pop	300 mL	6 for $1.49	(750 mL)	$0.33 ea
Bread	*same price* 500 g	3 for $1.45	750 g	2 for $1.45
Soap	100 g	2 for 63¢	(150 g)	3 for 99¢

• Working with ratio
• Building consumer awareness
• Using the calculator judiciously

42

3-33

Batter Up!

What are their batting averages?

Fill in the table.
(The calculations for the first line are shown below the table.)

Name	Hits	Times at Bat	Batting Average
Jones	84	304	0.276
Berstein	95	310	0.306
Duncan	83	340	0.244
Washington	96	295	0.325
Kew	26	141	0.184
Park	37	162	0.228
Brown	121	351	0.345
Kolinski	134	400	0.335
Sauvé	85	304	0.280
Totals	761	2607	**Team Average** 0.292

Jones' Batting Average = Hits ÷ Times at Bat
= 84 ÷ 304
= 0.276157
= 0.276

1. Which player would be the best one to have on your team? Explain your choice.
   Brown: Highest average (Also see *Teacher's Guide*.)

2. Can the team average be found in two ways? Explain.
   See Teacher's Guide.

3-35

Faster Than a Speeding Snail

Processing data with your calculator

This is a table of top running speeds of humans and various animals.

Animal	Speed (km/h)	Animal	Speed (km/h)
Pig	17.5	Greyhound	63
Quarter Horse	76.5	Gray fox	67.5
Rabbit	56	Grizzly Bear	48
Zebra	64	Human	45
Lion	80	Chicken	14.5
Garden Snail	0.05	Tortoise	0.27
Cheetah	112	Sloth	0.24

a. Arrange the animals in order of speed.

b. Find the ratios comparing the top speed of the animals with that of humans.

c. Put the result on the graph below.

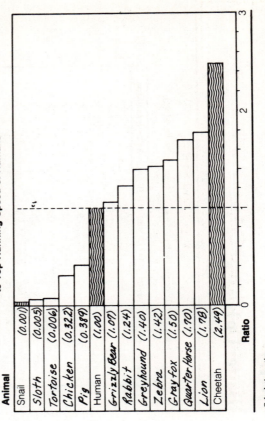

Ratio of Top Running Speed of Animals to Top Running Speed of Humans

Animal	
Snail	(0.001)
Sloth	(0.005)
Tortoise	(0.006)
Chicken	(0.322)
Pig	(0.389)
Human	(1.00)
Grizzly Bear	(1.07)
Rabbit	(1.24)
Greyhound	(1.40)
Zebra	(1.42)
Gray fox	(1.50)
Quarter Horse	(1.70)
Lion	(1.78)
Cheetah	(2.49)

Ratio   0   1   2   3

• *Calculating ratios*
• *Constructing graphs*
• *Using constants*

Sheet 3-34

Answers vary depending on the number of family members.

Name _____

45

3-38

Kool-Punch and Cake

These problems are easy with the calculator

1. Kool-Punch Stand

Bill's Kool-Punch stand was a gigantic success.

He sold $1.55 worth of drinks to 31 customers, and made a profit of 63¢.

a. What was the cost per glass? **b.** What is his profit per glass? **c.** What is the % mark-up?

5¢   2.03¢   68%

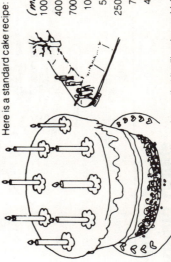

2. Largest Cake

The world's largest birthday cake weighed 11,365 kg.
Here is a standard cake recipe:

(mass of standard cake = 1532g)
100 g butter *741.84 kg*
400 g sugar *2967.36 kg*
700 g flour *5192.88 kg*
10 g baking powder *74.18 kg*
5 g salt *37.09 kg*
250 g milk *1854.60 kg*
7 g vanilla *51.93 kg*
4 egg whites (15 g each) *29,674 egg whites*

Based on this success, Bill opened a nationwide chain of Kool-Punch stands (Bill's Kentucky-Frozen Kool-Punch). If everyone in the country bought 1 glass on a particularly hot day, what would Bill's profit be? *Approximately*
$5,000,000

Rewrite the recipe so that it will make an 11,365 kg cake.

• *Finding ratios and percentages*
• *Working with metric quantities*

48

Sheet 3-36 and Sheet 3-37

Answers vary depending on the data collected.

3-39

Money Matters

A serious problem and two for fun

1. Up in Smoke

Find out the cost of a package of cigarettes. What would it cost to buy 1 pack daily for a year? For 40 years? (If the smoker lives that long!) *Answers will vary.*

For x-perts:

Check with a person who smokes to find out how many packs per day he or she smokes. Compute his or her smoking cost per year.

2. Heavy Expenses

Find the mass of a

penny:	_3.25_ g
nickel:	_4.5_ g
dime:	_2_ g
quarter:	_5_ g
dollar bill:	_1_ g

Calculate the mass of $100 in

pennies:	_32.5 kg_
nickels:	_9 kg_
dimes:	_2 kg_
quarters:	_2 kg_
dollar bills:	_0.1kg_

3. Discount Babysitting

Bill's Baby Business announces a special for November. Babysitting rates are $1.00 per hour for the first child, half of that for the second child, half of the cost of the second child for the third child, and so on.

a. Find Bill's rate per hour for 2 children. _$1.50_

b. For 3 children. _$1.75_

c. For 6 children. _$1.97_

d. What is his maximum rate per hour? _$2.00_

• *Collecting data*
• *Finding the mass of an object*
• *Conceptualizing a limit*
• *Finding rates*

Name _____

3-40

Round Things

Working with pi

Tire

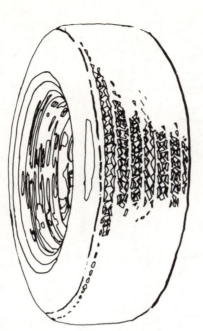

Belted Safety 40,000 km Treadwear-Rated

Cost: $37.50   Diameter: 83 cm

Cost per kilometer = _$0.0009375_

Number of revolutions required to go 40,000 km = _15,340,234_

Ferris Wheel Riding

The world record for ferris wheel riding is 21 d 3 h 58 min (i.e., 21 days, 3 hours, 58 minutes). During that time, the rider traveled 1158.728 km (in circles) in 11,800 revolutions.

a. What was the diameter of the wheel?
   _31.26m_

b. How long did the wheel take to travel 1 revolution?
   2.58min or 2min 35s

c. How long did the rider take to travel 1 km?
   26.25min or 26min 15s

d. What was the speed of the wheel in revolutions per minute?
   0.39 revolutions per minute

e. What was the speed of the rider in kilometers per hour? _2.28 km/h_

• *Working with pi*
• *Working with ratios*
• *Finding rates of speed*

Name _____

50

49

3-41
Moo!
Finding the larger facts

A certain hamburger chain claims to have sold 20,000,000,000 hamburgers.
The average hamburger has 100 g of meat, 2.5 mL of ketchup, and 0.3 g of salt.

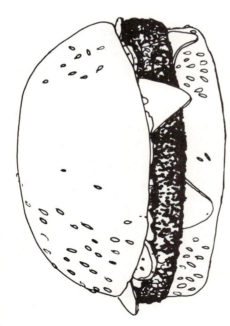

1. If a cow yields 150 kg of beef, how many cows were needed for these hamburgers? *13,333,333*

2. How many tanker trucks, each holding 6 m³, would be needed to deliver the ketchup? *8,334 (last truck only ⅓ full)*

For Experts
3. How many tons of salt were used? *6000 t*

Make up your own problem about the pickles found in some hamburgers.
Solve your problem.

• Working with large numbers
• Working with ratios

Name _____

51

3-42
From One Small Piece
It's easier than counting everything

1. Estimate:
a. the number of phones in this city: *50,000 (approx.)*
b. the population of the city (you'll need more information): *100,000 (approx.) If we assume there is one phone for every two people.*
c. the number of businesses in the city. *1000 (approx.)*

2. Discuss:
a. why your estimates may be inaccurate. *Small sample, poor sample (not random), etc.*
b. ways of making them more accurate. *Sample variety of pages, at random.*

Reprinted by permission of Johnson Publishing Company, Inc., Loveland, Colorado, 80537. ©1979 Johnson Publishing Company

• Sampling a large population
• Developing problem-solving strategies
• Working with ratios

52

Name _____

3-44
Remainders and the Calculator: Part I
What that decimal remainder means

1. Work out longhand. Leave a remainder. The first one is done for you.

a.
```
      7 R2
   4 ) 30
      28
      ‾‾
       2
```

b.
```
      4 R3
   5 ) 23
      20
      ‾‾
       3
```

c.
```
      5 R6
   8 ) 46
      40
      ‾‾
       6
```

d.
```
      9 R2
   4 ) 38
      36
      ‾‾
       2
```

2. Work out longhand. Use decimals. Check with your calculator. The first one is done for you.

a.
```
      7.5
   4 ) 30.0
      28
      ‾‾
       20
       20
       ‾‾
        O
```

b.
```
       4.6
   5 ) 23.0
      20
      ‾‾
       30
       30
       ‾‾
        O
```

c.
```
        5.75
   8 ) 46.00
      40
      ‾‾
       60
       56
       ‾‾
        40
        40
        ‾‾
         O
```

d.
```
       9.5
   4 ) 38.0
      36
      ‾‾
       20
       20
       ‾‾
        O
```

Compare **1a** and **2a**.
Think of a way to use the decimal quotient for finding the remainder.

```
    7.5
  ×  4
  ‾‾‾‾
   30.0
```

or

$7.5 \times 4 = (7 + 0.5) \times 4 = (7 \times 4) + (0.5 \times 4)$
$= 28 + 2 \quad$ Remainder
$= 30$

Think of a way to use your calculator for finding the remainder from the decimal quotient. Write down which buttons you push to check the remainder for (b). (c), and (d).

(b) ⬜ . ⬜6 ⬜X ⬜5 ⬜=

(c) ⬜ . ⬜7 ⬜5 ⬜X ⬜8 ⬜=

(d) ⬜ ⬜5 ⬜X ⬜4 ⬜=

• *Developing calculator algorithms*
• *Developing mathematical reasoning*
• *Reviewing inverse operations*

3-43
Friends
Working with patterns in numbers

1. Three people give each other Christmas presents. How many presents all together?
What if there had been 4 people? Fill in the chart.

For experts:

Can you find a formula that gives the number of presents for any group of people?
$n(n-1)$, *where n = number of people*

Number of People	Number of Presents
2	2
3	6
4	12
5	20
6	30
8	56
10	90
18	306

2. Three people are introduced to each other and shake hands.
How many handshakes all together? What if there had been 4 people?
Make a chart to show the number of handshakes for other groups.

For experts:

Can you find a formula that gives the number of handshakes for any group of people?
$\frac{n(n-1)}{2}$ or $1+2+...+(n-1)$, *where n = number of people*

Number of People	Number of Shakes
2	1
3 ·	3
4	6
5	10
6	15
8	28
10	45
18	153

• *Developing algebraic reasoning*

Name _____

3-45
Remainders and the Calculator: Part II
Decimals to remainders an easy way

1. Find the whole number remainder for the following:

$$6)\overline{39} = 6.5 \qquad 4)\overline{43} = 10.75 \qquad 5)\overline{62} = 12.4$$

R = 3   R = 3   R = 2

$384 \div 15 = 25.6$. What whole number remainder does the 0.6 stand for? __9__

2. Find a method for determining the whole number remainder without clearing the calculator.

Try: $434 \div 35$

Answer:

Whole number part:	12.4
Fractional part:	12
Whole number remainder:	.4 14

Your steps should be:

4 3 4 ÷ 3 5 = (12.4 − 1 2) × 3 5 =

Display

3. Write the quotient and remainder for the following.
The first one is done for you. Use your calculator.

	Quotient	Remainder
17 ÷ 2	8.5	1
23 ÷ 4	5.75	3
184 ÷ 16	11.5	8
200 ÷ 10	20	0
163 ÷ 8	20.375	3
4403 ÷ 136	32.375	51
1239 ÷ 42	29.5	21
6734 ÷ 185	36.4	74

· *Developing calculator algorithms*
· *Developing mathematical reasoning*
· *Reviewing inverse operations*

Name _____ 55

3-46
Remainders and the Calculator: Part III
Testing your skills with remainders

1. Multiply. Work out longhand.

$$\frac{1}{3} \times 3 \qquad \frac{4}{9} \times 9 \qquad \frac{2}{3} \times 6$$
$$= 1 \qquad\quad = 4 \qquad\quad = 4$$

2. Change to decimals.

$$\frac{1}{3} = 0.3 \qquad \frac{4}{9} = 0.4 \qquad \frac{2}{3} = 0.6$$

3. Repeat the questions of problem 1, using your calculator.

$$\frac{1}{3} \times 3 \qquad\qquad \frac{4}{9} \times 9 \qquad\qquad \frac{2}{3} \times 6$$
$$= 0.9999999 \qquad = 3.9999996 \qquad = 3.9999996$$

4. Compare the answers to questions 1 and 3. Which are right?

The answers to question 1.

> When the calculator shows 0.9999999, it usually means 1.

5. Find the quotient and whole number remainder for the following division problems.

	Quotient	Remainder
62 ÷ 3	20	2
73 ÷ 9	8	1
84 ÷ 13	6	6
127 ÷ 7	18	1
135 ÷ 19	7	2
236 ÷ 21	11	5
6087 ÷ 89	68	35
2111 ÷ 17	124	3

· *Developing calculator algorithms*
· *Developing mathematical reasoning*
· *Reviewing inverse operations*

Name _____ 56

Teacher's Notes